MAINSTREAM

MAINSTREAM

by

HAMILTON BASSO

REYNAL & HITCHCOCK · NEW YORK

PRINTED IN THE UNITED STATES OF AMERICA
BY THE CORNWALL PRESS, CORNWALL, N.Y.

For

Dominick and Louise Basso

Contents

About the Author

Hamilton Basso was born in New Orleans and it was there that he began his distinguished career as a journalist. In addition to writing for newspapers both north and south, he is a frequent contributor to leading magazines and the author of several novels, including *Courthouse Square* and *Days Before Lent*. Other than a biography of General P. G. T. Beauregard, this is his first work in the field of non-fiction.

INTRODUCTION

TO BE AN American is to be something new under the sun. One index to that newness, and not the least significant, is the difficulty of definition. Who is he, this American? The Boston Brahmin, the Allegheny mountaineer, the Louisiana Creole, the Ohio corn-and-hog farmer, the Pennsylvania steel-worker, the sons, grandsons, great-grandsons of a surge of immigrants from all over the world ——how is it possible to strike an average or a norm? One cannot, obviously. The happier inspiration would be not to try.

To speak of the American, then, is to speak of a mythical person; yet speak of him we must. It is a human habit, when dwelling on that which has no factual existence, an essence or an ideal, to resort to parables and symbols. The language of politics and business, in this respect, is at one with the language of mythology and religion. And our mythical American, without having his character tailored too much, can be made fairly representative of them all; because, however great the differences between individual Americans, however marked their points of dissimilarity, there is yet enough uniformity of thought and temper to set upon them the mark of an unmistakable family resemblance. They speak the same kind of language and their intellectual pockets jingle with the same kind of change. The Boston Brahmin and the Louisiana Creole, chancing to meet in a foreign country, will soon discover and recognize each other. Depth may call to depth, or shallowness to shallowness, but the recognition will be there.

If the American had belonged to a tribe of head-hunters, or

ix

to a race of African pygmies, this book, at best, would be only an inconsequential footnote to a vast body of literature. Our libraries would be full of books and monographs on the subject, bearing such titles as *The John Applegates: A Study Of Their Cults And Ceremonies* and *Einflüsse der Europäischen Zivilisation auf das Familienleben des Johannes Applegate*, and great men like Charles Doughty would have gone to live among them, sharing their lives and their hardships, and written great classics like *Arabia Deserta*. And, similarly, if a worker in anthropology should come across indisputable evidence that an Australian bushman and a Sioux Indian had met in hostile territory and shared a meal together, we would have a learned volume on the subject, full of notes and occult language, which would almost certainly gain its author an academic promotion and a raise in pay.

The encounter of our American friends, however, is hardly less remarkable, full of implications and hidden meaning which we, who in our American fashion take every miracle for granted, are apt to overlook. They might be seen as performers in a rather tremendous drama, acting out one of our basic American affirmations——that man is more than a tribal creature, that he can rise above the passions of blood-thinking, that he can live in peace and friendship with members of other tribes. (Always, of course, within the narrow limits of human frailty.) And so our travelers, instead of trying to tomahawk each other, or sitting in that higher stage of social behavior characterized by the smoldering hostility that might distinguish a similar meeting between an Italian and a Croat, (or, for that matter, a Frenchman and an Englishman) shake hands and start talking about business and the peculiarities of foreigners and the various excellencies of the United States. Each, in short, recognizes in the other some part of that ideal figment we call the American character.

II

The purpose of this book is simply stated. It begins with the assumption that there is an American character and that it has been shaped by a series of influences which, in their sum, may be taken to represent that other ideal figment we call the American tradition. It will be our hope to chart, as one might roughly chart a river-system, the larger tributaries in whose various mergings we see the mainstream of the tradition, and to indicate how these, in turn, have helped shape the American character. We have not sought any especial completeness, knowing our limitations, and also knowing that a fully detailed map of the system, down to the last minor headwater, is beyond the reach of a single cartographer. Like La Salle going down the Mississippi, we can only hope to indicate the general shape and current of the stream. And if, at the end, we seem to have overlooked rivers as seemingly important as the Missouri while giving undue attention to others as small as the Clinch, it must be put down to the temperament and prejudice of the explorer. For these, naturally, he does not apologize.

It may be well, indeed, to emphasize the matter of prejudice if only because it is so generally concealed. The central prejudice behind this book is a prejudice in favor of people. We are more interested in the human condition of our hero, whom we have named John Applegate, than in making use of him, for example, as a convenience to illustrate the theory of economic determinism. It would be futile to deny that John Applegate, like all Americans, has been enormously influenced by many economic forces. But what about the influence of P. T. Barnum? In the making of Americans, in the creation of that which we call the American character, which has been more important——the House of Morgan or the House of

Tom Thumb? Our tendency, or prejudice, would be to emphasize the latter.

This prejudice, as might be suspected, has had its effect on method. Aware that we are dealing largely with abstractions, and believing that a parable may often contain more illumination than a column of figures, it has seemed helpful to create a kind of false simplicity by illustrating the tendencies under consideration with biographical examples wherever possible, or, if not that, to take in general a biographical view. But here, again, no large completeness has been sought——it is a lack of ambition, rather than the presence of that admirable quality, that the author would like to stress. For he understands, only too well, that the full story of the American is quite beyond his telling; his or any man's. Poets, novelists, critics, philosophers, historians——all have applied, and still apply, their minds and their imaginations to the matter. And all of them, more or less, have ended where they began——caught in a spell and wondering still.

HAMILTON BASSO.

WHAT IS AN AMERICAN? From what does he draw his many tolerances—and his deep-laid prejudices? What are the sources of his cynicism—and his blind loyalties? What makes him every man's friend in the smoking-car —and a bottle-throwing maniac in the bleachers? Hamilton Basso imagines a typical American—John Applegate—and presents him as the true son of the most fascinating ancestors any man ever had. He tells us of Cotton Mather and John Smith, of Thomas Jefferson and P. T. Barnum, of Abe Lincoln and Teddy Roosevelt, of Andrew Carnegie and Huey Long. He shows how these and many others created the culture which has made John Applegate different from every other national on earth.

The emphasis is, however, biographical and interpretive. Illustrating the tendencies under consideration whenever possible with biographical examples, the author has written condensed but full-fashioned portraits of a gallery of significant Americans. The lives of these Americans are not regarded as isolated biographies but as part of an inter-related pattern which, as finally revealed, may be taken to be the design of the American character. By thus combining the methods of the historian, the biographer and the novelist, Mr. Basso has made a rich contribution to Americans' understanding of themselves.

"My boy, you've got to know the *shape* of the river perfectly. It is all there is left to steer by on a very dark night. Everything else is blotted out and gone."

"How on earth am I ever going to learn it, then?"

"How do you follow a hall at home in the dark? Because you know the shape of it. You can't see it."

MARK TWAIN: *Life On The Mississippi*

· 1 ·

COTTON MATHER AND JOHN SMITH
The American in the Beginning

IT IS A pleasant evening in June. The time, while close enough to be the present, is already part of the past. John Applegate, who owns and operates a corner drugstore in a small American town, is sitting at home alone. His wife and two children have gone to the movies. Had the picture not been one of those comedies his son calls "screwball," which he has never learned to appreciate, he might have gone with them; his taste runs to out-of-door dramas in technicolor, especially those that have a biographical or historical foundation, and to those lavish song-and-dance spectacles that remind him, a little nostalgically, of the musical comedy he saw in New York the year the Independent Druggists' convention was held there.

After a hard day at the store, its regular routine somewhat complicated by the presence of a young woman demonstrating a new kind of beauty cream, John Applegate finds it restful and pleasant to be alone. He is fairly tired, as is only natural for a middle-aged man who has been on his feet all day, and it is good to be sitting in a pair of old slippers with the little touches of home and comfort all about him——the new radio at his elbow, the family portraits on the upright piano, the latest edition of the adventures of Superman lying on the sofa where Sonny left it, Emily's college textbooks stacked on the table near the new novel she brought home that afternoon from the lending library.

Filling his pipe, John Applegate permits himself a sigh of contentment. Neither an arrogant nor an unctuous man, in fact a rather modest one, he can look back over the labor of his life and call it good. It is true the times are dark, and a pall of uncertainty hangs over the world, but John Applegate has no real doubts concerning his future or that of the country in which he lives. His confidence is not the same kind of confidence he knew in the years before the Great Depression, the memory of which lies like a raw and ruinous scar across his American optimism, but his faith is still enormous.

This faith is something his critics, his foreign critics in particular, have never been able to understand. To them it is fatuous at best: at worst, childish and absurd. What they fail to comprehend, though this is not the whole explanation of American optimism, is that John Applegate comes by it naturally. It is a direct inheritance from his pioneer ancestors. For whatever else was borne in the wagon trains that creaked across the plains, what hopes or dreams or failures or remembrances of past folly, an essential part of every cargo was a faith in the future——new hopes, new horizons, new fortunes, new times. And if, at journey's end, there were to be new follies and new failures, new regrets, there were always further and further horizons to be tempted and explored. Somewhere, somehow, someday——the face of America was the face of promise. The future lay ahead.

John Applegate's forebears, moving into the western wilderness, brought almost nothing with them save themselves. They cannot be called a people without memories, but even their memories were new. Time and the Atlantic Ocean had so thoroughly cut off two generations of Americans from the Old World that, as the wagons rolled onward, it was already a new and different people moving into a new and different land. The past, in the historical sense, did not exist for the pioneer. It was something he had slipped and was glad to slip

——inferior, exhausted, outworn. A pilgrim on the road to a new Mecca, Walt Whitman was his prophet.

> Have the elder races halted?
> Do they droop and end their lesson, wearied over there be-
>   yond the seas?
> We take up the task eternal, and the burden and the lesson,
>   Pioneers! O pioneers!

> All the past we leave behind,
> We debouch upon a newer mightier world, varied world,
> Fresh and strong the world we seize, world of labor and the
>   march,
>   Pioneers! O pioneers!

John Applegate is the son of his fathers. He, too, has left the past behind. To the despair of Europeans, and those of his countrymen who are sometimes oppressed by a feeling of spiritual emptiness, he finds it dull and tiresome to think about old patterns of culture and old ways of life. He has reached the age when a misty affection obscures his earlier years, making them seem all warm and golden as if hung with an Indian summer haze, but the past extends no deeper than that——no farther than the time when, as he likes to tell Sonny, you could catch a whole string of trout in the pool just beyond the big gray rock in less than an hour's time. The larger, deeper, richer past touches him not at all——or, at best, only when he finds himself being wooed by Hollywood's version of *Mary, Queen of Scots* or the storming of the Bastille. He is convinced, in his heart, that the new is better than the old. Can the first horseless buggy compare with the models now rolling from the assembly line? Would anyone trade this year's radio for a crystal set? To John Applegate's mind, the questions answer themselves. For while the last geographical frontier may have been reached, he is convinced that there are no limits to the frontiers of man's imagination. Here, in

America, the world will see such marvels as have never been seen before. John Applegate believes this as much as he believes anything. He is, as George Santayana has observed, an idealist working on matter.

Such idealism, however, rooted in contentment and an uncritical idea of what the future must bring, cannot help but be occasionally shaken and jarred. The conditions of John Applegate's life are vastly different from those of his grandfather's——more varied, more complex, harder to understand. In the days of the Conestoga wagon the forces that made for failure or success, for war and peace, for prosperity and depression, were not so complicated as to be beyond the reach of individual exploration. Thomas Jefferson, like John Milton, might reasonably think it possible to master the whole body of useful knowledge. With John Applegate, however, it is different. There are many things which, as he freely admits, are "over his head"; he sometimes feels caught in an enormous complexity. As a result he prefers things to be "simple," put in terms that "the average man" can understand; and, like millions of his countrymen, he is in unconscious revolt against the spiritual aridity of his time.

There are moments, then, more and more frequent of late, when he finds himself slipping into uneasiness and doubt. One such moment comes when, settling more comfortably in his chair, he opens the evening paper and turns on the radio.

The voice that comes over the air is not unfamiliar to him. It belongs to a Senator from a Southern state whose election to office was accomplished largely by means of a hill-billy band and the distribution of half-pound sacks of corn meal. Since his elevation to what Sonny's textbook on civics still calls the highest deliberative body in the world, the Senator has won further distinction by permitting himself to be photographed kissing a blond and bosomy screen star on the Capitol steps, the occasion being Washington's birthday, and by riding down Pennsylvania Avenue on top an elephant's head. John Applegate has followed his antics with a certain amount of amusement, having come to the unintentionally cynical conclusion that the Senate, like the old gray mare, is not what she used to be, and, besides, he does not have a high opinion of the political acumen of Southerners. Witness, for example, Huey P. Long.

Of late, however, the Senator has been appearing before the nation in a more serious role. It is not that blond screen stars and elephants have fallen off in publicity value; it is more that the Senator, living in Washington where the bacteria of ambition flourish so abundantly, has his eye on the Presidency. He is demanding more stringent immigration regulations. The present laws, he contends, are far too lax. Uprooted by the tremors that are rocking the old world, hordes of foreigners are swarming into the country: they threaten, he declares, not only American jobs, but the American way of life. Something must be done. All good Americans—one hundred per cent Americans, the Senator adds—should write to their representatives in Washington at once.

John Applegate does not agree with the Senator, having managed to rise above the down-pull of racism and blood-thinking, but even in his disagreement it never occurs to him to ask what the Senator means by a good, patriotic, one hundred per cent American. He knows. The Senator is addressing him personally. He means John Applegate and all the people like him. And the real American, the kind the Senator is talking about, is first and foremost a Protestant Anglo-Saxon. This concept is fixed in John Applegate's mind with the inviolability of quartz.

He knows, of course, as well as anyone, that there are millions of Americans who do not fall within this definition. There is, for instance, the agreeable young man who teaches athletics at the high school—his parents were Polish. John

Applegate understands he is an American, and occasionally suspects him of having a deeper appreciation of the meaning of America than some members of the neighborhood's "older" families, who are likely to take its promise for granted, but still the habit of defining the American in Protestant and Anglo-Saxon terms manages to persist. Nor does it ever occur to him, for one reason and another, that as early as 1782 these terms had lost whatever value they might have once possessed.

"The American," wrote Hector St. John De Crèvecoeur in that year, "is neither an European nor the descendant of an European; hence that strange mixture of blood which you will find in no other country. I could point out to you a family whose grandfather was an Englishman, whose wife was Dutch, whose son married a Frenchwoman, and whose present four sons now have four wives of different nations . . . Here in America individuals of all nations are melted into a new race of men whose labors and posterity will one day cause great changes in the world . . . They will finish the great circle."

The terms that John Applegate would use to define the American are thus some two hundred years out of date. It cannot be questioned, then, but that prejudice has helped shape his idea of the American——prejudice as useless as his appendix but just as likely to become inflamed. More than prejudice is involved, however, just as more than provincialism is involved in the mountain preacher's belief that when St. Paul went to Athens it was a citadel of culture and learning almost as important as Asheville, North Carolina. In saying that the American is Protestant and Anglo-Saxon, John Applegate has compressed the history of several centuries into what he regards as a simple statement of fact. If his synthesis is incorrect, or if he has made history mean what he wants it to mean, he is no more at fault than have been innumerable historians. It is true of John Applegate, as it is true of men generally, that his observations are more likely to shed more light on his own character and personality than on that which is being observed.

II

All history, Ernst Toller slyly tells us in his play *No More Peace*, is the propaganda of the victorious. To John Applegate, always distrustful of barbed cleverness, this would sound like heresy. Although he does not read history, except in his newspapers, he does not think it should be made fun of. That would be trifling with a subject which, like sex and Thanksgiving, he considers rather sacred. Unlike his daughter Emily, who knows more about George Washington's false teeth than she does about the battle of Lexington, he does not like to have his heroes painted, as did Cromwell's followers, "warts and all." Any attempt to convince him of the element of truth in Toller's observation——by pointing out, for example, that Benedict Arnold might be remembered differently had the colonists lost their revolution——consequently would be futile. He accepts his view of history as he accepts the credit of his customers——on trust. It has never crossed his mind that his concept of the American, irrespective of any incidental propaganda, has been determined largely by the two forces, Protestantism and Anglo-Saxonism, that have been most dominant in the United States up to the present time. Nor has he paused to realize that it rests principally on priority, or that his psychology is not unlike that of those travelers who, boarding an ocean liner at Hamburg, used to consider themselves old inhabitants by the time they reached Le Havre; looking down upon those who came aboard there as brash and noisy newcomers, ignorant of language and having no sense of tradition.

His view is a partial one at best, leaving out much more than it puts in, yet, to support it further, John Applegate might cite the larger span of American history——in his view a strictly Anglo-Saxon affair. He knows that the continent he lives upon was discovered by the Norsemen, and brought to the later attention of the world by an Italian in the service of Spain, but this he tends to regard as two unimportant accidents, easily preventable had the proper Englishmen been around.

He knows, also, about the Indians. One of his great-uncles, Truslow Applegate, rode with the Indian-fighter John Sevier who later became the first governor of Tennessee, and another was with Winfield Scott when the Cherokees were defeated at Wayah Gap in the Great Smoky mountains. Not long ago John Applegate made a pilgrimage to the place where his latter ancestor won his captain's promotion. He had a real pioneer's feeling, he said, as he rode up the new road that leads to the top of Wayah Bald and looked out over the tumbling ranges fixed in a silence as inviolate as time. The thing he most vividly remembers, however, is the visit he and the family made to the Cherokee reservation. He was frankly disappointed. There were better, more realistic Indians to be seen, as he told Sonny, with the old Wild West shows—— Buffalo Bill's in particular. There was a feeling of sadness, even of pathos, he had not anticipated. He left the reservation in a complicated frame of mind. The Indian, he felt, must have suffered a considerable decline since the days of Pocahontas and Captain John Smith.

This Captain Smith has had a greater effect on John Applegate's thinking, especially in relation to his concept of the American, than ever he imagines. Up until the time Captain Smith arrived in Jamestown on that eventful May 13, 1607, the American scene, as far as John Applegate is concerned, was a stage without actors——the Indian being less real and substantial than the trees of the forest through which he moved, a tobacco-smoking wraith who pilfered his enemy's scalp and used, in his benighted fashion, shells for money. It took a man like John Smith, John Applegate would say, a Protestant Anglo-Saxon, to get things really started——an opinion, incidentally, that is shared by all the Applegate connections, especially the Virginia branch of the family, many of whose daughters bear the name of Pocahontas.

Nor does it matter that most of the Applegates, and John in particular, know little about Captain Smith except that Pocahontas risked her neck for his. Or did she? Captain Smith, in a passage that suggests the terse prose that *aficionados* of the Eighteenth Century admire so much in Daniel Defoe, assures us she did; but then, as his book of *Travels* reveals, he had a lifelong habit of getting himself rescued at every serious juncture by a beautiful female of high estate. It happened, by his own count, five different times.

We cannot help but wonder what John Applegate would say to this side of his hero's character: this, not lady-killing exactly, but a curious genius for arousing womanly sympathy in bosoms Italian, Turkish, Muscovite, French and American Indian by turn. But, in any case, John Applegate's admiration of John Smith is not misplaced. Hot-headed, making enemies more readily than friends, Smith was nonetheless the only early colonial leader who fully understood the reality of the struggle in Virginia and who grasped the essential nature of the colonial economy. His departure from Jamestown, brought about by an explosion of gunpowder that sent him back to England for medical attention, nearly caused the colony's ruin; only the arrival of a new expedition saved the settlement from complete disaster.

Asked for gold when he returned to London, he gave his superiors something better——a map of the region, a sound survey of its resources, and the sort of good sense about colonization that fills his little book, *Advice For the Inexperienced Planter*. It would be too much to say that without John Smith the English venture in America would have failed; it is not too much to say that he was one of the greatest contributors to its success. And so, in a sense, John Applegate is correct. It did take a man like John Smith, a Protestant Anglo-Saxon, to get things really started.

III

If John Applegate knows little of Captain John Smith, he knows even less about Cotton Mather. Yet this New England divine, as complex a character as America has produced, not without a certain tolerance of people when they honored and obeyed him but calling them "insignificant lice" when they did not——this intensely emotional man who knew burning visitations and wild exaltations, nervous and irritable, the most widely-read person of his generation, has had a far greater influence upon John Applegate, and his America, than can ever be credited to the quarrelsome little captain who liked to be got out of trouble by tender-hearted women.

Having been said so often, it must be said again: any inquiry into the American character, no matter how modest, must look into the causes of what has been called "the pronounced singularity of temper and purpose" that distinguished the New England settlements, and, with equal emphasis, the earlier New England character. This temper and purpose, it need hardly be said, is what has come generally to be known as Puritanism——something, to John Applegate, vaguely associated with the gloomy figure in the tall black hat used by cartoonists to represent Prohibition during the time when the Bill of Rights did not contain the right to drink a bottle of beer, and the cause, to those of his intellectual peers who make the same mistake of reading history backwards, for the general "lack of color" and "repression" of American life: a conclusion possible, it would appear, only to such analysts as are willing to draw large conclusions from meager samplings of evidence, and who have never visited Coney Island, or Main Street, for that matter, on Saturday night.

Puritanism, more easily derided than defined, can only be described as the philosophy of life and the set of values that was taken to New England by the first settlers in the early Seventeenth Century. As such, it has been one of the most persistent of those several continuous philosophies and traditions, such as the rational liberalism of Jefferson and the Hamiltonian view of conservatism and government, that have been woven into the fabric of American life. Even Franklin D. Roosevelt and his New Deal, long separated in time from John Winthrop and the charter of Massachusetts Bay, were to be considerably influenced by it——the Puritan believing, despite his recent invocation in favor of free enterprise and *laissez-faire*, in government regulation of business, price-fixing, and the taxing of excess profits. John Cotton, the grandfather of Cotton Mather, condemned in 1639 as a "false principle" the theory "that a man might sell as dear as he can, and buy as cheap as he can," and in Winthrop's *Journal* it is recorded that one Robert Keayne was assessed £200 by the General Court and called to account by the church of Boston for making a profit of sixpence or more on the shilling.

There is, within the space of this essay, no room for an adequate consideration of the secular and religious movement that was Puritanism. Of the Puritan fathers, however, about whom both too much and too little has been written, two simple things may be said. Their thinking was almost entirely dominated by the thinking of John Calvin, whose *Institutes Of The Christian Religion* became the chief basis of Protestant theology until the Nineteenth Century, and they were completely opposed to that form of government known as democracy.

There is a close connection between the two. The bigotry that lighted the pyre of Servetus, who anticipated Harvey in his theory of the circulation of the blood and who was condemned as a heretic by Calvin, was to flare again in Massachusetts when the witches met their deaths. The doctrine of predestination, formulated by the Geneva dogmatist, and his emphasis upon an authoritarian system of government, were to help shape the society of those tight little New England dicatorships that have come to be regarded, collectively, as the cradle of American democracy.

John Applegate, knowing so little of the religious influences that helped shape the character of colonial America, for Puritanism was but one of the several forms in which the Calvinist version of Protestantism was brought to the New World, cannot be said to have forgotten much. He has simply not had time nor inclination to discover that the Puritan theocrats, nearly all as harshly Calvinistic as Calvin himself, came to America, not to set up a new and happier kingdom of man, as he is wont to imagine, but a new and stricter kingdom of God. The quest was indeed a quest for liberty, and behind it lay a flaming zeal, but it was not the liberty that is generally associated with the American way of life. Many things were carried across the waters in the *Mayflower*, but not the idea of democracy.

What was brought, primarily, was a highly elaborate and codified philosophy which, remaining fairly rigid in its orthodoxy until the middle of the Eighteenth Century, had as its social ideal the establishment of a church government modeled upon the example of the Apostles in the New Testament, and presided over by a small and highly learned ministry. Religion, to the Puritan, was more a thing of the head than heart ——a very complex and extremely intellectualized affair, comprehensible only to theological experts trained and educated with all the care a more secular century would later lavish upon its chemists and engineers. The Puritan considered the Bible an absolute code in everything it touched upon; he held it plain and explicit enough so that men, or men with the proper training, could establish its authority on every subject ——ethics, war, taxes, inheritances, profits, clothing, diplomacy and law included.

As for democracy, was there a democracy in heaven? Were not the celestial spheres ruled by an hierarchy of superior beings? Could it be held that the redeemed sinner, saved only by the grace and mercy of God, was on the same footing of equality with the supernatural Himself? Merely to have asked such questions would have meant exile or imprisonment. Roger Williams, the first and finest of American liberals, was cast out for less.

John Cotton put the matter plainly enough. "Is it better," he inquired, "that the commonwealth be fashioned to the setting forth of God's house, which is his church, than to accomodate the church frame to the civil state? Democracy, I do not conceive that ever God did ordain as a fit government either for church or commonwealth. If the people be governors, who shall be governed? As for monarchy and aristocracy, they are both of them clearly approved, and directed in scripture."

Only one more step need be taken, the merging of this doctrine with the Biblical explanation of the fall of man, and the doctrine of the elect——the right, that is, of the elect to rule——becomes not only correct, but sanctified; a thesis later to be restated in different terms, and with varying definitions of the elect, by Alexander Hamilton, John Calhoun, Mark Hanna, and various proponents of the modern feudal state. To Hamilton, speaking in a moment of anger to Jefferson, the people were "a great beast"; in the eyes of the Puritan theocrats they were hardly less beastly——stupid, carnal, burdened with sin, doomed to eternal damnation. When Cotton Mather denounced them as "insignificant lice," he was voicing, along with his wrath, an opinion to which he had been educated since childhood——the belief, in general, of the theocratic elect.

IV

Cotton Mather was the third member of a dynasty as important to early Massachusetts as were the Medici to Florence. Had he been born in the shadow of Giotto's campanile, and been christened in the cathedral of Santa Maria del Fiore under the name of Lorenzo by his uncle the Cardinal, he could scarcely have been more distinctly branded. His name itself is like a coat-of-arms indicating his position in Seventeenth Century New England, carrying the same implication of authority as the five red balls, and the single blue one adorned with the lilies of France, that identified the leading family of the Italian Renaissance.

On his father's side of the family, Cotton Mather was a grandson of Richard Mather, the first minister of Dorchester, and on his mother's of John Cotton, the dominating figure in the councils of the early New England clergy and one of the most highly esteemed men of his time——"one," said Cromwell, "whom I love and honor in the Lord."

His father, Increase Mather, was the outstanding member of the second generation of New Englanders. Educated at Harvard, Increase then studied at Trinity College, Dublin, taking his degree in 1658. He then saw a brief period of semimilitary service as chaplain to the garrison at Guernsey, returning to Boston in 1661 after the Restoration blocked his hope of any further advancement in England. The next year he married Maria Cotton, daughter of John Cotton, and, as teacher of the Second Church in Boston, found himself strategically located to influence the civil affairs of the colony. In 1685 he became president of Harvard College and three years later returned to England on a diplomatic errand, remaining abroad until 1692 while negotiating a renewal of the colony's charter. His influence at the time of his home-coming was so great that he was able to nominate the governor and the whole slate of magistrates; after which, for reasons which today are more dull than important, his power began to decline.

The life of Cotton Mather, who has come to represent the arch-embodiment of the Puritan, was contained within much narrower limits than that of either his father or grandfather. Born in 1663 to the clerical purple, and conscious of it as any Tuscan princeling who ever swaggered the streets of Florence, he never got beyond the borders of either orthodoxy or Boston——together they made his world. There were but faint stirrings of tolerance in John Cotton, who first gave countenance to the teachings of Anne Hutchinson and then recanted in the face of hostile opinion, and none at all in Increase Mather, an unyielding autocrat who sought to reforge old tyrannies in an age that was anxious to cast them off, but in Cotton Mather, blood of the theocracy's blood, bone of its bone, the inquisitorial nature of the Calvinist system is brought to its harshest and most disagreeable extreme.

Educated at home by his father, Mather entered Harvard at the age of twelve, taking his M.A. when he was eighteen. Ordained the colleague of his father at the North Church in Boston, he married the first of his three wives in 1686, and soon became one of the outstanding leaders of orthodox religious opinion in eastern Massachusetts. Made a fellow of Harvard College, he hoped and expected to become its president, but when his father was forced to resign that post, and another appointed, he resigned his fellowship and gave himself over to his clerical and literary activities; publishing, in his sixty-six years, some five hundred books, tracts and pamphlets, the greater proportion of them on ecclesiastical subjects.

One of the remarkable things about Mather, or one thing about him that would seem remarkable, is that not once, in all his long life, does he permit himself to be liked. There is a certain charm to John Cotton, who seems to have been a Caroline gentleman as well as a Calvinist, and while it is hard to be fond of Increase Mather, it is at least possible to respect him——there still burned a few last embers of the early Puritan fire: there was yet some understanding of the frailties and necessities of men.

"Drink," Increase said in one of his sermons, "is in itself a good creature of God, and to be received with thankfulness, but the abuse of drink is from Satan; the wine is from God, but the Drunkard is from the Devil."

In the cramped opinion of Cotton Mather, however, all that was from God was wrath: all else lay within the kingdom of Satan——a province that held his imagination in perpetual thrall. "I have set myself," he wrote in his diary, "to countermine the whole Plot of the Devil against New England, in every branch of it." Even as a child, the pampered darling of Boston, "learning to pray as soon as he could speak," he seems to have dwelled on a decidedly abnormal plane. To have entered Harvard at twelve, the youngest student ever to be admitted there, is perhaps in itself no evidence of abnormality; but the flaming visions we find recorded in his diary, those torments of angels and demons that remind us of the water-colors of William Blake and the paintings of Hieronymus Bosch——these must be accepted as evidences of an unhealthy mind.

Modern medicine would agree with William James, at least in part, when he says in his *Varieties of Religious Experience* that some persons are born with an inner constitution which is harmonious and well balanced from the start——a happy "internal climate," in the phrase of Claude Bernard. Others, as James continues, are oppositely constituted, and are so in degrees which may vary from something so slight as to result in a merely odd or whimsical inconsistency, to a discordancy of which the consequences may be inconvenient in the extreme. We have here a range, then, broad enough to include persons all the way from Mrs. Annie Besant and Carrie Chapman Catt, through Tolstoi and Dostoevsky, down to Cotton Mather and St. Louis of Gonzaga——the odd, the discordant, the extreme.

Mather's chances of being born with a harmonious constitution were more than ordinarily slim. From both sides of his family he inherited a highly-strung nervous system that was further aggravated by his own precocity and that gruelling twelve-hour intellectual regimen, made part of family tradition by his grandfather, called "the scholar's day." And that to this physical maladjustment there was added a psychological disharmony, to a degree that would seem extreme, is more than suggested by the pages of his diary——he is too tensely on guard, for one thing, against "lascivious thoughts" and "wanton imaginings." The following entry, made in his twenty-second year, is not without its own kind of illumination, especially if we remember Mather's close identification of himself with God.

Casting my eyes upon the gentlewoman who carved for us.	Lord, carve of thy graces and comforts a rich portion unto that person.
A gentle woman lately married.	Lord, espouse and marry the soul of that person unto thyself, in a covenant never to be broken.
A gentlewoman very beautiful.	Lord, beautify the soul of that person with thy comeliness.

It is true that these "ejaculatory prayers," as Mather called them, were also offered up for a tall man (that he "might have high attainments,") a lame man, (that he "might walk uprightly,") and a Negro, (that his "soul might be made white in the blood of the Lamb.") Gentlewomen and young gentlewomen, however, do seem to have been of special and compelling interest—not in itself proof of anything, for woman being the weaker and therefore more dangerous sex might have needed more praying for than man, but another bit of evidence to suggest that the female image, so often confused with the image of sin, must often have burned like one of his flaming visions in the forehead of the night.

Beyond this, however, in the complex of Mather's character, lay something much deeper and far more terrible—fear. And it is fear, as we may learn from a study of Ivan Pavlov's experiments in the field of conditioned reflexes, that is much more fundamental than sex to the genesis of neurotic manifestations. This conclusion of Pavlov's—which, incidentally, was established in the laboratory—was fully confirmed durin the War of 1914-18 when more major neuroses could be seen in a week than in a lifetime of ordinary investigation. It was the emotion of fear, not sex, that was the basis of all those palsies, contractures, tremblings, contortions and epileptiform seizures. Sex, as Pavlov proved, is an occasional incitant to action; fear a constant and daily one.

Mather, throughout his life, on page after page of the voluminous record he left for us, insisted upon his love of God and upon himself as a beacon of righteousness in the dark night of man's mortal error and sin. Righteous he was; but the flame of that righteousness was not love. Mather had love neither for man nor God. It was fear that seized and cramped him, that lay behind his railing, his scolding, his shrill egotistical rancor. Over his head there hung the same predestined sword, forged in the furnace of Calvin's imagination, that he dangled over the heads of "these fallacious people," "these obnoxious men," "these recalcitrant sinners." Mather thought he was one of those who would be saved; but did he know? He wanted to do God's work, yes; but, more than that, in the narrows of his soul, he wanted to be spared the rod of vengeance when the day of Judgment came. "Save me! Save me!" he cried——not once, not twice, but over and over again: and the terror in his voice comes plainly down the years.

That all of this should have produced an abnormality, a distortion and a crookedness of view, is not to be wondered at; the wonder would have been otherwise. "A malcontent priest," a contemporary called him, one consumed with "an heriditary rancor" that made him everlastingly opposite to every will but his own. Rectitude, admittedly, has always been part of the New England character; but rarely was rectitude ever carried to such distortion as this. There was an egotism to Mather that led him to believe, not merely that he was right, but that his was the only rightness in an otherwise totally wrong-headed world——an egotism that would recur, with certain mutations, in one of his most distinguished spiritual descendants, John C. Calhoun of South Carolina.

"The monstrous and crying wickedness of this town!" Mather cries out in his diary. "A town at this time strangely possessed with the devil. And the vile abuse which I do myself particularly suffer from it. These things oblige me, in the fear of the divine judgements, to fall down before the Lord, in most earnest supplications for his pity and pardon to a people so obnoxious to his displeasure."

Torn from its historical context, this might seem an impassioned supplication not markedly different from hundreds of others. It is only when we understand that it was written at a time when Mather had aroused the antagonism of Boston by advocating inoculation as a precaution against smallpox, and had been hooted in the streets, that its psychological suggestions come clear. This is the one time in Mather's life, when he is trying to combat the hostility born of ignorance, that he might be admired. But the antipathy of the people to his proposals becomes, unfortunately, "the monstrous and crying wickedness of this town"; they are possessed, not of backwardness, but of the devil himself. And finally, having incurred the displeasure of Cotton Mather by their "vile abuse," it automatically follows that they have incurred the equal displeasure of the Lord.

The pages of Mather's diary are thick with epithets flung at his enemies; they strew the pages like jagged glass. And there are times when it seems he thought himself the only man in Boston not "strangely and fiercely possessed of the devil" or given over to "violent and impetuous Lusts." And his passion for self-magnification, for spreading his name and reputation, is almost beyond belief. Let a nameless wretch of a girl be hanged for killing her illegitimate child, and, after preaching the execution sermon, he rushes into print with his *Pillars of Salt*—"an history of Criminals executed in this Land, and of my own Discourses with them in their last Hours." Let a witch be put to death, and once again the itch for publication quickens his pulse and blood: the dissertations on witchcraft crowd each other on the printer's hook. So it happened throughout his life. He doubtless considered his books, the whole procession of them, as pious tributes to the Lord. They are seen more clearly, today, as burnt offerings to Cotton Mather.

Even the one avenue through which an apologist of this stone-age Puritan might escape, by seeing him as an example of piety carried to excess, is blocked by the high stone wall of his egotism. The essence of piety is self-immolation. Mather was too militant a churchman, too fierce in his pride, too aggressively self-centered, ever to justify his being regarded as belonging, even honorarily, to that fraternity of abnegated souls who seek peace and saintliness by a renunciation of the world. Cotton Mather in a monastery? One might as well try to imagine St. Francis on Broadway. And yet, for all the differences that lay between the Thirteenth and Seventeenth centuries, Mather managed to bridge them. Is not his theopathic righteousness strikingly reminiscent of the psychopathic saintliness of St. Gertrude, a Benedictine nun whose *Revelations* are a well-known mystical authority, and which consist largely of confessions of Christ's fondness for her unworthy person? And does he not also suggest St. Theresa—her voluble egotism, her love of giving instruction to those less fortunate than she, her consciousness of a host of "faults" and "imperfections" which, as in the case of Mather, did nothing to interfere with her excellent opinion of herself? In such a comparison, however, Mather comes out second best. St. Theresa, as William James noted, had a splendid intellect, wrote excellent descriptive psychology, possessed great talents for politics and business and, above all, was gifted with a buoyant disposition and an admirable literary style.

To read of the lives of the saints, and then to read Cotton Mather, especially his *Wonders Of The Invisible World*, is to realize that his mind was a well of mediaevalism——an anachronism in its own time. He too was to become an anachronism, almost a living ghost, and in his old age when the shadow of failure and bitterness darkened his life, he was to see the rising impetus of a new age, less dominated by theological ideals, lap about the foundations of the temple he and his fathers had built. He revered that temple, for the days of his life were as stones lifted into its structure, and he would not believe that its rooms were too cold and cramped for men to live in. Self-righteous to the last, taking in his latter years to fasts and vigils, he died in Boston on February 13, 1728. His last hours would have been brightened, one believes, if he had known how long and how deeply the tradition of which he was the arch-exponent was to influence the larger tradition of

American life. He seems now, a primitive figure out of a primitive past; yet his voice, in certain places when the wind is right, may still be listened to, scolding and railing across the land.

John Applegate has heard echoes of that voice in many places—in school, in church, in politics, in business. The Protestantism of his Anglo-Saxon American, the one hundred per cent American so beloved of the Senator on the radio, is heavily charged with the Calvinistic Puritanism of New England. As Captain John Smith may be taken to represent racial heritage, so may Cotton Mather be taken to represent religious tone. An able colonizer with a talent for being rescued by high-placed women (if he was so rescued!) and a rancorous clergyman who believed in demons and witches. These are the two pillars, strange as it might seem to him, upon which John Applegate's concept of the American finally rests—a concept so unrealistic, so void of understanding and illumination, as to be given denial at every turn. To trace the larger definition of the American is to trace, in part, the course of the American mainstream—a swelling torrent that gets broader and deeper as it goes along until, like the ruined timbers of Cotton Mather's theocratic temple, the narrow framework in which John Applegate would confine the nature and character of his countrymen is also swept away.

· 2 ·

FAREWELL AND HAIL TO
THOMAS JEFFERSON
The American As Democrat

ACLIMATE and a culture lay between Puritan Massachusetts and Cavalier Virginia. The Anglican gentlemen who imposed the social structure of Seventeenth Century England upon the great tobacco plantations of Eastern Virginia had little in common save speech and racial ancestry with the God-fearing burghers who bent their backs to the cat-o-nine-tails that was Cotton Mather's tongue. To leave Mather's diary for the diary of William Byrd of Westover, the second of a line as important to Virginia as was the Mather family to Massachusetts, is like leaving a cold bleak region where the sun rarely shines and crossing into a greener, warmer country where frailty is understood to be a human condition and not a mark of the damned.

Diaries, by their very nature, are the most revealing of all literary compositions; a secret diary like Byrd's, kept as was Pepys' in a private shorthand, is apt to be revealing to the point of discomfort. The traditional and idealistic view which sees Cavalier Virginia as a land of refined elegance and William Byrd as the personification of its grace and culture, for example, cannot help but be shaken by his forthright statement that the beds in Colonel Dudley Digges' house stank; or by his telling us that, on the evening of a ball planned in honor of the Queen's birthday, Governor Spotswood had to bribe his servants into staying sober by promising they could all get drunk the next day. It is hardly necessary to remark that neither, the condition of the beds nor the behavior of the servants, could have happened in Massachusetts. Nor could William Byrd have happened in Massachusetts. A different moral, social and geographical climate was necessary to bring about the flowering we discover in his diary.

"We ate milk and strawberries for breakfast," he noted on May 22, 1710. "Then we played at billiards till about eleven o'clock when Mr. Woodson came to see me. We ate cherries and talked of many things. I ate beef for dinner but ate too much. In the afternoon we drank some tea and ate more cherries. In the evening I took a little walk with my wife. I was out of order with eating too much."

The entry for November 2, 1709, has a further illumination. "In the evening I went to Dr. Barret's where my wife came this afternoon. Here I found Mrs. Chiswell, my sister Custis and other ladies. I played at (r-m)* with Mrs. Chiswell and kissed her on the bed till she was angry and my wife also was uneasy about it, and cried as soon as the company was gone. I neglected to say my prayers, which I should not have done, because I ought to beg pardon for the lust I had for another man's wife. However I had good health, good thoughts and good humor, thanks be to God Almighty."

One beef-eating squire lording it over his manor, the owner of more than 179,000 acres of the best land in Virginia and a library of four thousand volumes, schooled in Latin and Greek, but not above wenching with chambermaids, ("About 3 o'clock I returned to my chambers and found a girl above who I persuaded to go with me into my chambers but she would not.")——such a man does not establish the full character of a society any more than does a malcontent cleric haunted by devils in the night. William Byrd, however, may

---

* The exact nature of this particular pastime has apparently eluded the decipherist of Byrd's diary.

be taken to be as fairly representative of Cavalier Virginia as Cotton Mather was of theocratic Massachusetts. That they were poles apart needs no further stressing; it is so obvious that the important meaning is likely to be missed——as, indeed, it has been. Different they were. It is intriguing to think of the flying of sparks that would have attended their meeting. But, for all their differences, for all the hostility that would have lain between them, they would have been in complete agreement, (except, perhaps, on point of definition) on one basic issue: the right of the elect to rule. Mather, railing at the "monstrous wickedness" of Boston, and Byrd, whipping his servant Lucy for her "impertinence," were both acting from the same central conviction. They were the elect and their right to rule, God-given on the one hand, wealth-given on the other, was not to be questioned.

The elect of Virginia, however, gentlemen of William Byrd's wealth and station, were relatively few. Seventeenth and early Eighteenth Century Virginia is not to be thought of as a community of large plantations owned by rich men. Except for the settled areas on the eastern shore, it was largely frontier country that had just reached the agricultural or "small clearing" stage. The great majority of the inhabitants had come at their own expense, receiving fifty acres for each member of their families, and others had arrived as indented servants, either voluntarily or under sentence of the courts. The typical land-holding was small, approximately two-thirds of the owners had no slaves, and by the close of the Seventeenth century three generations had not pushed beyond the fall line, a point reached as early as 1675. It was not until the turn of the century, when a colony of French Huguenots formed a settlement on the James just above the falls, that the Piedmont was opened.

The Piedmont, a geographical term that has given us an easy way of dividing the Atlantic coastal plain into two re-

gions, the other being the Tidewater, may be used in our
present consideration as a fairly accurate synonym for the
frontier; and it was the frontier, over and over again, that was
to dispute the theory, sometimes with violence, that the elect
had the right to rule.

Since we are not formal historians, and may indulge in the
pleasure of speaking relaxedly, we can say of the frontier
that it was a boundary, an experience, and a state of mind.
Of the influence of the frontier upon America, and upon
Americans like John Applegate, we need not entirely subscribe to the views of Frederick J. Turner to agree with his
general idea.

"At first," he wrote, "the frontier was the Atlantic coast.
It was the frontier of Europe in a very real sense. Moving
westward, the frontier became more and more American.
Thus the advance of the frontier has meant a steady movement away from the influence of Europe, a steady growth of
independence on American lines."

It was not Turner, however, who first saw the frontier as
a prime determinant of the American character and the American way of life. That credit belongs to a Frenchman, Hector
St. John de Crèvecoeur, whom we have already mentioned
and whose *Letters From An American Farmer* exercised considerable influence upon Eighteenth-Century opinion in America. This Crèvecoeur, one of those interesting but minor figures generally relegated to the purgatory of footnotes, was a
man of education and breeding, an ex-soldier and explorer under Montcalm in Canada, who emigrated to the American colonies around 1760. After living for a time in Pennsylvania, he
moved to the state of New York, married a Miss Mehitable
Tippet of Yonkers, and settled down on a 120-acre farm in
Orange County. Out of this agricultural experience came his
two volumes of *Letters*.

Crèvecoeur, having eyes to see with and a head to think

with, was an economic determinist some one hundred fifty years before that phrase became part of our intellectual slang. "Men are like plants," he wrote in a passage of shrewd Gallic earthiness. "The goodness and flavor of the fruit proceeds from the peculiar soil in which they grow. We are nothing but what we derive from the air we breathe, the climate we inhabit, the government we employ, the system of religion we profess, and the mode of our employment." This habit of looking upon men as plants, upon social systems as vegetable mold or manure, upon immigration as transplantation, gives a freshness and liveliness to his letters that in no way interferes with the shrewd clear thinking that goes on beneath. In one place, speaking of "the middling and the poor" that emigrate to America, he has this to say:

> "In Europe they were as so many useless plants, wanting vegetable mould, and refreshing showers; they withered and were mowed down by want, hunger and war: but now by the power of transplantation, like all other plants, they have taken root and flourished! . . . By what invisible power has this surprising metamorphosis been performed? *Ubi panis ibi patria* is a motto of all emigrants. Here the rewards of his industry follow with equal step in the progress of his labor; his labor is founded on the basis of nature, *self-interest*; can it want a stronger allurement?"

No great subtlety is needed to discover, in this final sentence, the germ of the "rugged individualist" thesis which became, long after the circumstances that gave it validity had vanished, the dominant political doctrine of the Coolidge-Mellon-Hoover era. But Crèvecoeur, being under no obligation to try to conjure away a complicated industrial and financial dilemma by repeating a simple phrase, explored beyond the economic individualism of the frontier and asked himself a more important question: what happens to the transplanted European when he sends down his roots in a new and fertile soil?

"The early knowledge they acquire," he wrote, "the early bargains they make, give them a great degree of sagacity. As freemen, they will be litigious. As citizens, it is easy to imagine that they will carefully read the newspapers, enter into every political disquisition, freely blame or censure governors and others. As farmers, they will be careful and anxious to get as much as they can. As Christians, religion curbs them not in their opinions."

It was obvious, even to Crèvecoeur, that such a class of men would not willingly submit to any considerable abuse of privilege on the part of established authority; he had Bacon's Rebellion, flaring in Virginia a full century before the Revolution, to give confirmation to his belief. American democracy, as has been said, was born of no theorist's dream; it was not carried in the *Susan Constant* to Virginia, nor in the *Mayflower* to Plymouth. Nor did it spring from the New England town-meeting. It came out of the frontier, not as doctrine but as human experience, and it was a frontier intellectual, Thomas Jefferson, who gave it its largest and finest statement. Not, however, that the Declaration of Independence was as the morning sun warming the field of domestic liberty. America, as Carl Becker has observed, was free before it was independent; it was free because Americans had hewn out their own freedom in a new country. Democracy, as a political philosophy, came considerably after the fact. It derives, not from the Constitution, which is to our political ethics as the Ten Commandments are to our moral creed, but from the body of experience accumulated in the wilderness. And it was Thomas Jefferson who, more than any other American of his generation, embodied the ideals that fired and lighted the great revolution. It was given to him to speak the American challenge——the people, not the elect, have the right to rule——and his life was a declaration of his faith. To think of America is to think of democracy; to think of democracy is to think of Jefferson. He is the father of the American waters.

II

John Applegate, sitting in his living-room listening to the radio, peacefully unaware that he is living out the last few months of an historical era, remembers Thomas Jefferson—— when he remembers him at all——as a rather grim-lipped man who stands holding a quill in the center of a steel engraving portraying the signing of the Declaration of Independence. Even a pilgrimage to Monticello, made on the same junket that took him to the Great Smokies and the Cherokee reservation, failed to bring the quill-holder to life. He could not agree with Sonny who said that Jefferson must have been "a wacky sort of guy," or with his daughter Emily who called him "one of the convenient references of American folklore," but he did feel that the Sage of Monticello had a curious preoccupation with gadgets that reminded him of his second cousin Obadiah who was always "inventing" something. Had he been told that the various ingenious devices to be seen at Monticello were but the playful experiments of a man whose imagination also conceived a swivel chair, a pedometer, a machine for treating hemp and a radically superior mold board——that part of the plow which turns the earth——he would have been impressed. More, he would probably have felt a certain kinship; for the mind of Thomas Jefferson, like that of John Applegate, might also be called the mind of an idealist working on matter.

To say this, however, is to skirt the problem and indulge in an easy evasion. One of the most complicated figures in our history, an idealistic humanist grained deep with the spirit of scientific inquiry, an enlightened Puritan who delighted in

France with all the enthusiasm of the intellectual, a political philosopher who was also one of the shrewdest of practical politicians——all this makes Jefferson impossible of any easy summing-up. Like Scripture, passages from his life may be taken to illumine almost any text, and, as a result, he has come down to us in a hundred different guises from whoremonger to saint. A happy hunting ground for those in search of their doctorates, the subject of a thousand painstaking papers on Jefferson the Gardener and Jefferson the Architect and Jefferson the Parent, he is the only American of major greatness who lacks a capably definitive biography. Despite his far-reaching influence, the endless citing of his words and works, the nature and significance of his philosophy is only now beginning to be understood. Indifferently consistent, rigging his sails to catch the shifts and humors of every wind, he seemed to his enemies a man without promise or principle, a devious rabble-rouser who gained the mob in order to further his own demagogic ambitions. And, at the outer boundary of the other extreme, to those who loved him he had no faults, being almost as a lanky long-limbed deity come to walk the earth for a time and share the fitful dreams of men.

For all this——the cultism and the calumny, the deification and the abuse——there is more than ordinary excuse. Of all great Americans, Jefferson is one of the hardest to reach. There was a central theme to his life, basic and consistent, but on that theme he wove many variations. It is not always easy to tell the variations from the theme. He left us, unfortunately, save for the inadequate *Notes On Virginia*, no systematic formulation of his thoughts that might serve as a score. "A life of constant action," he wrote, "leaves no time for recording." This, however, was an exaggeration. He found time, otherwise, to record his thoughts on almost every subject under the sun.

One of the characteristics of John Applegate, bound to his

set of conventional responses, is that he always sees his heroes in those moments that contain the pinnacles of their careers. The great moment of Jefferson's life he would say——and here we would agree with him——came when he wrote the Declaration of Independence. John Applegate thinks of it, correctly, as a great historical and political document. But it is more. It may be taken, especially in the first sentence of that resonant second paragraph that has colored all subsequent American thinking, either in affirmation or denial, as one of the most revealing biographical statements Jefferson left for us.

We hold these truths to be self-evident: that all men are created equal; that they are endowed by their Creator with certain unalienable rights; that among these are life, liberty and the pursuit of happiness.

The pen paused, the candle guttered in a draught, the moment was big with history. Behind the young man with the quill——sandy-haired, loose-jointed, his careless dress doing little to modify a certain stiffness that was always to be something of a barrier between him and other men——lay thirty-three years of personal experience. Where, in the soil of those years, had the seeds been dropped that now, germinated by the hot sun of rebellion, were bearing such signal fruit?

The planter, the principal sower of seeds, it is generally held, was John Locke; the Declaration, in word and phrase, discloses his influence. So it does. Concerning the influence of Locke's thinking, during those vulnerable early years when Jefferson was at college in Williamsburg, we need not disagree. The disagreement is larger and more central to a deeper issue. The theory that would establish John Locke as the governing authority of the Declaration conceals, in its neatness, a highly dubious major premise. It would make the charter of our independence a purely intellectual achievement, all head and no heart, kin to one of those modern blueprints of the future conceived in the apparent illusion that the use of an engineering phrase somehow establishes the authority of scientific accuracy.

Jefferson came a little nearer the mark. His intention, he wrote retrospectively to Henry Lee, was "not to find out new principles, or new arguments never before thought of, but to place before mankind the common sense of the subject in terms so plain and firm as to command their assent." The Declaration, he continued, "was intended to be an expression of the American mind," depending for its authority "on the harmonizing sentiments of the day, whether expressed in conversation, in letters, printed essays, or in the elementary books of public right."

In another letter, written to John Cartwright in 1824, he goes more deeply into the matter:

"Hume, the great apostle of toryism, says 'It is belied by all history and experience that the people are the origin of all just power.' And where else will this degenerate son of science, this traitor to his fellow men, find the origin of *just* powers, if not in the majority of the society?

"Our Revolution commenced on more favorable ground. It presented us an album on which we were free to write what we pleased. We had no occasion to search into musty records, to hunt up royal parchments, or to investigate the laws and institutions of a semi-barbarous ancestry. We appealed to those of nature."

Nature. Always, when it comes to a question of final authority, as it does here, Jefferson turns to nature for support. But where, in nature, could he have found a rational basis for his belief? Is it not possible, dispassionately, to find equal argument for the opposing opinion of that "degenerate son of science," Hume?

The answer, as Jacques Maritain suggests in his luminous essay, *Human Equality*, is that Jefferson, while convinced he was giving statement to an empirical fact, was actually voicing an article of faith. It is not the equality of men, but their inequalities, that are to be empirically observed. Such inequalities cry out; they cover the whole expanse of reality. It is only by transcending the intellect and the senses, as Maritain says, that we may discover and participate in the nature or essence which all men have in common, the total equality which lies in their communion in the mystery of the human species.

Jefferson, who in a letter written to his acquaintance Van der Kemp in 1816 rejected the concept of the Holy Trinity because no man ever had a "distinct idea" of it, would have had little patience with any such mysticism as this. All his life he was to ponder the matter, seeking proof of the equality of man in nature just as other rationalists of his century sought proof of the existence of God, and not once does he seem to have recognized it for what it was——a flower plucked from the fields of faith.

John Applegate, like Jefferson, would be made uncomfortable by this. He likes to believe that the cornerstone of his American system is made of more durable stuff. The word faith disturbs him, suggesting idolatry and superstition, and he has never thought through to the fact that moral principles lie at the root of every society. And yet, though he has never read a word of philosophy or been remotely troubled by the quarrel about universals, he too has pondered the question of the equality of men. Are they created equal or are they not? He finds it hard to say. To answer in the affirmative demands an act of faith, a projection beyond the empirical process, and this is something that goes against his dry Scotch-Irish grain. He is conscious of a conflict, a tugging at cross-purposes. Some meaning, obscure and difficult, will not come clear.

Nor did it ever come clear to Thomas Jefferson. The lean

scholar of Monticello is, in many ways, a discouraging man to live with. It takes no great generosity to agree with those who see him as a kind of Renaissance man, a lesser Leonardo da Vinci, but, generosity and admiration to the side, there are times when we might wish he had done some clearer and harder thinking about the Declaration of Independence. Jefferson the Gardener and Jefferson the Architect and Jefferson the Musician are interesting to know about, and each important in his field, but these facets of a many-sided man shine no light on John Applegate and do not point his way. The great accomplishment of Jefferson's life, as John Applegate instinctively senses and Abraham Lincoln clearly saw, was in introducing an abstract truth, an ethical and spiritual principle, into what would have otherwise been a mere revolutionary document. This, apparently, Jefferson never realized. The argument of democracy, as he left it, depended too much on sentiment and emotion. Apparently finding himself unable to say that all men are created equal because each man has a soul and is therefore equal in the sight of God, thus rejecting a metaphysical view that a later generation would also be prone to reject, he permitted himself to be drawn into that ambiguity of thought, which he confused with rationalism, that has been one of the most pronounced characteristics of liberal democracy from that day to this.

No documentary evidence has as yet been uncovered to show that Jefferson ever read a line of Rousseau, whose theory of the natural goodness of man came to him in the form of a vision, as he tells it, but it is clear that early in life the Virginian fell under the influence of the new ideas, largely flowing from the French philosopher, which during the Eighteenth Century were modifying the thought of the world. The various conflicts we find in Jefferson, as in his opposing ideals of the "natural equality of men" and a "natural aristocracy of talent and virtue," are traceable, in part, to a conflict between Puritanism and Rousseauism. Although he professed agreement with Condorcet, "that man's mind is perfectible to a degree of which we cannot as yet form any conception," there is no reason to conclude, as have some of his more uncritical admirers, that he embraced unreservedly the Rousseauian idea of the natural goodness of man. Sincerely loving the people, Jefferson nonetheless had a lively suspicion of them—they could be trusted, as he makes abundantly clear in his remarks on education in the *Notes On Virginia,* only within definitely circumscribed limits.

In the end, however, it is the Rousseauist in Jefferson who gains the upper hand. The Puritan's vision of the natural depravity of man is supplanted by a modified version of Rousseau's vision of man as naturally good. "I cannot act," wrote Jefferson in this regard, "as if all men were unfaithful because some are so . . . I would rather be the victim of occasional infidelities, than relinquish my general confidence in the honesty of men." This is a warm and generous view, one that made him a constant champion of the people, but it rests on no natural "law" whatsoever. Alexander Hamilton, turning to the same field of observation as Jefferson, and no less intellectually brilliant, could find enough support of the Puritan view to support his own "confidence," at least in a political sense, of man's natural depravity. It is of course true, as Jefferson's writings make clear, that his hope for democracy did not rest on the concept of man's "natural goodness" alone. This idea, however, was so central to his architecture, so essential, that should it be removed, as John Calhoun was to prove, the whole structure stood in danger of tumbling down.

To say that there were certain failures in Jefferson's thinking is not to detract from his greatness. He gave a nation its idealism and its creed, not once was he to veer from his belief in the worth and dignity of the common man, and if he helped bring about the modern confusion born partially of the substitution of Rousseau's dualism for the older dualism of Christianity——the one seeing man's natural goodness as thwarted by the evil of society, the other looking upon good and evil as being contained and opposed in the heart of man——we are yet profoundly in his debt. Perhaps, as John Adams charged, in the Declaration of Independence he invented nothing. His words, however, still burn and crackle in our sky.

Too much a child of his rationalist century ever to admit the irrational content of his thought, Jefferson was likewise too narrowly confined within the limits of his own hope and experience ever clearly to perceive the dangers that threatened his vision of society. The framework of that society, the broad landscape of the world he hoped to see, is contained in his *Notes On Virginia*——a little book which John Applegate has never heard of, and from which we may deduce, if we care to load the dice, that Jefferson had never heard of the Industrial Revolution. It would be an error, however, as Charles Beard has written in his essay *Jefferson and the New Freedom*, of which the next several paragraphs are a paraphrase, to assume that the swing of human activities that were giving rise to modern industrialism was not observed by so keen a man as Jefferson. The factories of New England were already being driven by water power, and steam engines were throbbing in England, when the Declaration of Independence was flung out to the world. In his *Notes On Virginia*, written in 1781, Jefferson shrewdly observed the tendencies of European states to foster manufacturing, and, after a careful examination of the rising financial system, came to several basic conclusions as to its meaning for the United States. Almost as if the new industrial capitalism did not exist, the goal of his analysis was an agrarian democracy——a good and even a noble goal, but one based on the theory that the New World must continue to be a thinly settled agricultural community with the greater proportion of its citizens engaged in tilling the soil.

"While we have land to work," he exhorted, "let us never wish to see our citizens occupied at the work-bench, or twirling a distaff."

After some searching reflections on the relation of economic independence to civil liberty and republican government, Jefferson reached the conclusion that only farmers, owning their own land and working it with their own hands, could possess that independence of character, the self-reliant sense of right and responsibility, which he saw as the guardian of democracy. Whoever depends upon the "casualities and caprices of customers" has set upon him, no less than Cain, the mark of corruption. The tillers of the earth are the favorite children of God, while those who do business in the market place or labor for others in factories are on the downward path to that moral decay which marks the end of democratic freedom.

It is well to let Jefferson take the floor and speak for himself: "Generally speaking, the proportion which the aggregate of other classes of citizens bears in any state to that of its husbandmen, is the proportion of its unsound to its healthy parts and is a good enough barometer whereby to measure its degree of corruption." Of wage-workers he had this to say: "Let our workshops remain in Europe. The mobs of the great cities add just so much to the support of pure government as sores do to the human body. It is the manners and spirit of a people which preserve a republic in vigor. A degeneracy in these is a canker which soon eats to the heart of its laws and constitution. . . . I consider the class of artisans as the panders of vice, and the instruments by which the liberties of a country are generally overturned."

These, as Beard points out, were no angry outbursts. They were the reasoned convictions of a mature and determined man. We do Jefferson an injustice, however, just as those who ignore the above remarks do him a greater injustice, if we overlook their origins in place and time. The formative years of Jefferson's life were spent on the frontier, in what has been called the first West in American history, and while his mother was an aristocratic Randolph, he was also the son of a plain husbandman who was one of the first settlers to move into the Virginia Piedmont.

Peter Jefferson, the father of Thomas, was an interesting person in his own right. A land surveyor and Indian fighter, vigorous, thrifty, used to what the Appalachian mountaineers call "the roughs and the toughs" of life, he brings to mind two of John Applegate's favorite characters——Davy Crockett and Daniel Boone. Employed to survey the southern boundary of Virginia, he took advantage of his opportunity and patented several thousand acres for himself; settling upon it in 1737 "to grow up with the back country." He made his way well enough to find favor with Isham Randolph of Dungeness and marry one of his daughters——thus giving those who lean to the Shinto side excuse and opportunity to look upon his son Thomas as one born to the manorial purple.

Young Thomas was put to school with a Scotch pedagogue whose modest house of learning was situated in Louisa County ——at that time the home of rising radical democracy and stubborn Presbyterian dissent. Louisa County was a place where men wore buckskin breeches, coonskin caps, and hunting shirts without coats to cover them. It was a hunter's country, filled with turkey and fox and deer, and one of the Jeffersons' neighbors, a youth from Hanover named Patrick Henry, had already made a reputation for himself with his "long hunts" and rollicking ways.

Aristocratic Virginia centered in and around Williamsburg. Here were the winter houses of the great planters who came to attend the sessions of the Royal Council when the burgesses assembled, and here, when he was seventeen, young Jefferson arrived to attend the college of William and Mary. Much has been made of the few years he spent in Williamsburg.

They were indeed a cultural influence, buffing the young backwoodsman to a cultivated shine, but one wonders, considering the mores and manners of Cavalier Virginia, if the humble origins of his father might not have been a source of difficulty and hurt. Such depths of his character cannot be plumbed. We know only that he brushed aside the Randolph claim to an imposing pedigree that went back to Queen Mary, and gave his earliest sympathies to the people with whom he had lived as a boy——the small farmers along the upper rivers, the tobacco-growers on their modest freeholds, the hunters and trappers of the Allegheny slopes. The idealisms that moved him, then and later, were the idealisms of the frontier ——its faith in human kind, its belief in economic individualism, its hope that here, in a new country, the lot of the common man could somehow be made happier than it was.

More, however, than Jefferson's youth was involved. When he wrote the *Notes On Virginia* he was almost forty. He had watched America change from a jealous group of bickering colonies into a united sovereign state and he was convinced that the change, in itself a drift toward the bigness he was always to distrust, was filled with danger for the common man. He had looked at Europe and the lessons of Europe and he understood how the movement toward bigness, from simplicity to complexity, from freedom to regimentation, might lead straight to the establishment of the monolithic state. He had no illusions about Leviathan. It was not above swallowing man and his freedom as, in the Bible, it swallowed the hapless Jonah. Everywhere he went in Europe he found wretchedness and poverty and they seemed to him inevitable consequences of the highly centralized state. Political tyranny was but the visible extension of a human tyranny whose cancerous threads ran through the whole body of society. The monolithic state, resting on the authority of police-power, was merely the handy instrument through which this dual tyranny, political and human, could most easily be maintained. There is a note of homesickness in many of his letters from France, between whose lines we can read his vision of America——an agrarian society of free men exploited by neither an aristocracy nor a plutocracy——and these shed further light on the rejection of industrial capitalism contained in the *Notes On Virginia*.

"You are perhaps curious to know how this new scene has struck a savage from the mountains of America," he wrote his Italian friend Bellini. "Not advantageously, I assure you. I find the general fate of humanity here most deplorable. The truth of Voltaire's observation offers itself perpetually, that every man here must be either the hammer or the anvil. It is a true picture of that country to which they say we shall pass hereafter, and where we are to see God and his angels in splendor, and crowds of the damned trampled under their feet."

America, happily, was different from Europe. The tyrannical police-power of the old world state had here withered to a mere village arrangement intended to keep the rural peace. Each citizen had, or could reasonably hope to have, a small stake in the economic order. Private property, in Jefferson's opinion, was one of the essential conditions of freedom—— democracy cannot rely on noble sentiments or good intentions; it must have some solid foundation. Any centralization or collectivization of the national economy, even a substantial part of it, threatens to undermine the democratic base.

Believing this, and all the modern admirers of Leviathan have merely obscured his arguments, not answered them, the rejection of capitalist industrialism contained in the *Notes On Virginia*, was a natural and inevitable consequence. Not to have rejected it would have meant a denial of all the lessons of experience. He sprang from a simple agrarian society and he wanted to preserve that society. It was a simple world he lived in, with a simple domestic economy——a small world, also, in which nearly all the people were plain rural folk, living on farms or in little villages, with no shocking contrasts between wealth and poverty and no sharply defined class cohesions. He himself would not have called it a pure democracy: there were restrictions on suffrage, and the gentry owned slaves, but there was solid reason to believe that the country was steadily progressing toward a more democratic order.

There was the bright star, also, of education. "Of all the views of this law," he wrote in the *Notes On Virginia*, "none is more important, none more legitimate, than that of rendering the people the safe, as they are the ultimate, guardians of their own liberty. . . . Every government degenerates when trusted to the rulers of the people alone. The people themselves, therefore, are its only safe depositories. And to render even them safe, their minds must be improved to a certain degree. This indeed is not all that is necessary, though it be essentially necessary."

It was a good world he lived in, rich with promise and with hope, and he loved it too much willingly to thrust it aside. To gut the good green earth, to raze the forests and poison the rivers, to crowd a people into such dark foul slums as he had seen in Europe, to open the door and bid Leviathan welcome ——how could he? He may be charged, correctly, with being blind to the larger forces of his time. For this, however, it is easy to forgive him. Blindness is one of the conditions of love.

But what of John Applegate? He lives in a country whose very heartbeat is the pulsing of the machine. Its society is based upon the "casualties and caprices" of trade and more than half of its people belong to the "mobs of the great cities." What message has the Sage of Monticello for him?

We can only follow Jefferson's thought to its farthest projection and then guess. When he was seventy-three, long after he had written the *Notes On Virginia*, his views of industrialism had been modified. His years in the White House, coinciding with the Napoleonic wars that brought hardship and ruin to neutral shipping, had convinced him of the need of domestic manufactures. "We must now place the manufacturer by the side of the agriculturist," he admitted, "or else become a mere agricultural colony of Europe." Beyond this, however, he did not go. Unlike his great opponent Hamilton, he was apparently unable to understand the dynamics of the Industrial Revolution, or that, once begun, it could not be checked or halted but must run its course. It is futile, consequently, for John Applegate to look to Jefferson for a political philosophy or program applicable to an industrial age. That, however, does not mean he has nothing to say. There is enough evidence to believe that he might have turned away from the contemporary scene in horror and dismay (Monticello is in itself such a piece of evidence) but if we keep in mind the central theme of his life, we may perhaps surmise his probable attitude toward our manufacturing society.

The harsh brutality of our great industrial centers would have appalled him, and he would be hard put to recognize the tool-less, landless, traditionless factory worker as a source of democratic health, and having written to Charles Hammond in 1821 that "When all government, domestic and foreign, in little and great things, shall be drawn to Washington it will become as venal and oppressive as the government from which we separated," he would find his position as patron saint of the New Deal puzzling in the extreme. But his was an elastic mind, sensitive to the shifts and mutations of time, and while he may have grieved that his dream of America had gone down to ruin, he might have recognized the frontier of the machine as the modern extension of the frontier he knew in his youth. Whatever his criticisms, and they would be many, of one thing we may be sure: he would still insist that "government exists only to secure the welfare and happiness of its citizens," and, from this insistence, argue that it is the social and human side of the ledger that finally counts. And one thing more: one thing above all others. The people, not the elect, have the right to rule. Having never varied from this conviction, he would not vary now. He would speak to John Applegate, even as he spoke in correspondence with his friend Hartley in 1787, the credo that was his life:

"I have no fear but that the result of our experiment will be that men may be trusted to govern themselves without a master. Could the contrary of this be proved, I should conclude, either that there is no God, or that he is a malevolent being."

To admire Jefferson is not necessarily to love him. He gives off a light rather than a warmth. But stand on the ramparts of Monticello, where on a good day the hills of Albemarle fall away into what seems the ultimate country of man's content, and you know you are in touch with the democratic ideal. Here lived a man who loved freedom too much to deny it to anyone. This is his monument and this his fame. Nothing can detract, least of all the failure of his lost agrarian dream, from the inspiration of his life. The wilderness still hurls its challenge—"Nothing then is unchangeable but the inherent and unalienable rights of man"—and the fields of the republic spread out their promise beneath the long American sky.

· 3 ·

JOHN CALHOUN OF FORT HILL
The American As Aristocrat

THE SURGE of backwoods democracy that brought Andrew Jackson into the White House——(a person, incidentally, of whom Thomas Jefferson did not approve, calling him one whose passions were terrible, a dangerous man)——also brought to the Vice-Presidency for his second term a gaunt and commanding South Carolinian who, more firmly than Jefferson, was to plant himself like a granite dike against the rising tide of industrial ambition and, in his efforts to maintain and solidify an agrarian society, bring the nation to civil war and the very edge of ruin.

Just as Patrick Henry is a more vivid figure to John Applegate than Thomas Jefferson, so is Andrew Jackson more salient in his imagination than John Caldwell Calhoun. The man of action, the Indian fighter, the hero of the battle of New Orleans, the stormy petrel of the Presidency whose championship of an ex-barmaid was to create a national scandal——this exciting and nervous record makes one whose greatest accomplishment was a disquisition on government seem dull and dusty by contrast. But that disquisition on government was, in a sense, the rock on which the ship of the republic was almost to founder and go down. More important than that, in relation to its hidden influence upon John Applegate, it is the master beam of the fullest philosophy of the right of the elect to rule ever to be fashioned out of native American life and experience. Calhoun, animated by what he regarded as the

44

highest motives, but lured into sectionalism by bitterness and the persuasive ideal of a Greek democracy, was to borrow the general groundwork of Jefferson's thought and erect a superstructure of aristocratic affirmation that, in the end, would cause him to become representative of reaction.

Vilification, then, is easier than understanding——with Calhoun, perhaps more than with any other American, the good was interred with his bones. All parties, even those confused and over-enthusiastic idealists of the extreme left who would set life free by paralyzing all its vital impulses, seek justification for their policies in the writings of Jefferson. None dare admit their philosophy even to be remotely descended from the teachings of the great Carolinian. Yet Calhoun was generally regarded as the logical inheritor of Jefferson's mantle and when he died he was mourned by more Americans than even the Sage of Monticello. He walks across the American stage like a figure out of one of the old tragedies——haunted, not so much by fate, as by the more personal nemesis of his being. He dreamed of being the architect of a new kind of society and instead designed, room by room, the house of his own disaster.

In 1811, when American commerce was being plundered by English ships, the state of South Carolina sent to Congress a brilliant young quartet——John C. Calhoun, Langdon Cheves, David R. Williams and William Lowndes. It was largely at their insistence, added to that of other so-called War Hawks, that the war of 1812 was declared.

The dramatist or novelist already sees the obscure workings of chance and destiny. The Congressional debates that preceded the war of 1812 were swiftly to bring Calhoun to national attention; from that time on he was never out of the public eye. But the war itself lifted to even greater prominence Andrew Jackson who, by defeating the British under

Packenham at New Orleans, staked his largest and most dramatic claim to the Presidency that Calhoun was later to covet and, being denied it, suffer the canker of bitterness eating at his heart. So, at the very beginning, the dragon's teeth were sown.

Larger forces were also at play. There was no visible evidence that the long Virginia hegemony was sinking on the arc of afternoon or that the humanitarian idealism of Jefferson would soon be eclipsed by a markedly opposite creed. But even then popular opinion in the South was undergoing a revolutionary change. During the first two decades of the Nineteenth Century, pro-slavery opinion was passive. The first defenses that appeared were written in a tone of apology. A substantial part of the South had no love for the institution and those who took a realistic view——the advent of realism coinciding with Eli Whitney's invention of the cotton gin and the opening up of the vast Mississippi delta empire to the cultivation of the staple——preferred not to reopen a question they thought settled by the compromises written into the national constitution. But by 1820 apology began to shift to defense: the conviction was growing that the institution was too profitable to permit its extinction.

Remembered as the foremost apologist of slavery, Calhoun in this respect was but one member of a fairly sizeable company. The arguments in favor of the slave system had nearly all been put forward long before the institution was introduced into the plantation South. As ancient an institution as society itself, slavery early became a subject of philosophic inquiry. The greatest of Greek thinkers justified slavery as conforming to logic in nature; the law-minded Romans laid a basis for it in both the *jus civile* and the *jus gentium;* the patristic writers of the early Christian era endowed it with the sanction of church and religion. Aristotle, Ulpian, St. Augustine, St. Thomas Aquinas and Pufendorf were among those who contributed to the body of pro-slavery thought.

The defenders of the institution in the Old South drew freely from this heritage, revising and recasting the old arguments to fit the special circumstances of their particular case. And as the tone of their argument became angrier and angrier, passing from apology to defiance, it became increasingly clear to the agricultural imperialists that the fortunes of the South could no longer be trusted to the Virginians of the old tradition, and that leadership must pass to South Carolina. This meant, inevitably, that the reins of Southern policy be placed in the hands of John Calhoun. Between the state and the man there could be no separation. John Calhoun was South Carolina and South Carolina was John Calhoun.

II

The intellectual and social capital of South Carolina, in 1820 as today, was the city of Charleston. Calhoun came to represent Charleston, and is that city's most distinguished shade, but he did not begin there. Like Thomas Jefferson, he was an upcountry man.

The section around Abbeville, South Carolina, where John Calhoun was born in 1782, used to be called the Long Cane country. Settled by French Huguenots, Scotch-Irish and Germans who were granted tracts of land before the Revolution, it is a lonely region of small clearings and hillside farms lost in a forgotten corner of the world. Elizabethan archaisms still survive in the common speech, for the highlands of North Carolina are not far away, and there persists a belief in ghosts and witches. It is a country quick to violence, where politeness is the mannered courtesy of men who still go armed, and the sound of its music is the hill-billy whine and the belling of the hound-pack on the scent of a coon. Its scattered people live lonely lives, walled largely by the bounds of self, and when John Calhoun was born one year after Cornwallis' march through South Carolina it was more lonely still. He was to show the influence of that loneliness all the years of his life.

"The cast-iron man," Harriet Martineau called him; "one who looks as if he had never been born." And Mrs. Jefferson Davis, in her memoir of her husband, said he always reminded her of "a mental and moral abstraction."

The son of a farmer, growing up in the empty Long Cane country, Calhoun had no regular schooling for the first eighteen years of his life. Sent at the age of twelve to live with the family of his brother-in-law, a Presbyterian minister and school-teacher, he read with such avidity that his health became undermined. He returned to his father's home and, until he was nineteen, was put to the hard tasks of life on a frontier farm——a severe and monotonous regimen broken only by hunting and fishing expeditions. Then, his father deciding he might have another try at books, he returned to live with his brother-in-law, now head of a sizeable "log college" where the boys lived in small cabins, chopped their own firewood, planted their own food, studied ten hours a day and rested only on Sunday——the sort of place, altogether, that would have won the heart and blessing of Cotton Mather.

Two years of this stern Presbyterian discipline, plus an equally rigorous training in the classics, enabled Calhoun to enter the junior class at Yale. Life in New Haven under Timothy Dwight was only slightly less severe than life in the "log college." That Calhoun absorbed much of the learning and rectitude of New England is to be suspected——that the germs of his secessionist doctrine came out of Connecticut is somewhat more surprising. His residence in New England, however, fell during the time when some of the Northern opponents of the Jeffersonian regime were urging their section to secede from the unholy alliance (a movement that

finally culminated in the secret "Hartford Convention" of
1814) and it was during this period of political debate that
the seed of secession was first planted in Calhoun's thought.

His position then, interestingly enough, was anti-secession-
ist. Thomas Jefferson was his great ideal and it was characteristic of him to champion his hero against the rabidly Fed-
eralistic Dwight himself; causing the latter, it is said, to pre-
dict that his young opponent would someday sit in the White
House. Characteristic, too, was the subject Calhoun selected
for his commencement day address: "The Qualifications
Necessary to Constitute A Perfect Statesman."

The letters written from New Haven and Litchfield, where
he went to study law, are those of a man whose mind has
already fallen into its natural shape——dry, pragmatic, grace-
less. "We have excellent sleighing here," he wrote from Litchfield in 1806 to the Charleston lady who was to become his
mother-in-law. "I was out last evening for the first time this
season and found it very agreeable. It is a mode of convey-
ance that the people of this state are very fond of."

And to his friend Andrew Pickens: "You do me an injustice in supposing your letters intrude on my studious disposition; I am not so in love with law as to feel indifferent to my
friends. Many things I study for the love of study, but not
so with law. But, I confess, from my aversion to it, I draw a
motive to industry. It must be done and the sooner the better
is often my logick."

One of the effects of his delayed education, as Gamaliel
Bradford has noticed, was that he never learned to spell correctly. Even the letters written late in life are full of irregu-
larities. And one senses, from the beginning, a certain narrowness of range, a mind whose best recommendation is that it
is too conscientious ever to misrepresent what it finds. It is
only necessary to read the letters he wrote to Floride Calhoun,
the first cousin who was to become his wife, to believe the

story that while he once tried to write a poem, he could get no further than "Whereas——"

He read much and what he read he remembered, making it part of his own close-grained thinking, but apparently his books were nearly all of an historical and political nature. Nowhere does the difference between Jefferson and Calhoun, the polished frontiersman and the unpolished one, appear more strikingly than in the letters they wrote on the general subject of reading.

Jefferson, admitting the entertainments of fiction to be "useful as well as pleasant" goes on to say: "If the painting be lively, and a tolerable picture of nature, we are thrown into a reverie, from which if we awaken it is the fault of the writer. I appeal to every reader of feeling and sentiment whether the fictitious murder of Duncan by Macbeth in Shakespeare does not excite in him as great a horror of villany, as the real one of Henry IV by Ravaillac as related by Davila?... We neither know nor care whether Lawrence Sterne really went to France, or whether the whole be not fiction ... Considering history as a moral exercise, her lessons would be too infrequent if confined to real life."

And now Calhoun. "I would advise a young man with your views," he wrote to a correspondent in 1840, "to make himself thoroughly acquainted with the history of the free States of antiquity and the history of England and our country, and to read the best elementary treatises on Government, including Aristotle's, which I regard as among the best.* To this must be added a thorough knowledge of po-

---

* Calhoun's debt to Aristotle is apparent throughout all the South Carolinian's political writings, even though payment takes the form of denying most of Aristotle's conclusions. Calhoun's chief borrowing from Aristotle, other than his justification of slavery, would seem to be the concept of the *élite* as put forward in the philosopher's *Politics;* but here again Aristotle's final view, which denies the right of the *élite* to rule, is rejected by Calhoun in favor of his own contrary opinion.

litical economy, and of our country in all its relations, including its resources and the character of the people. But all this leaves much that can be acquired only by actual experience."

Jefferson certainly comes off the better of the two, writing with grace and charm, while the dry unleavened Calhoun seems merely to be advising his young correspondent to study less and experience more. Yet considering the nature of his own education, he could hardly have advised otherwise. Growing up on a frontier farm with solitude as his greatest teacher, he had learned to reason before he could read. He lived in the intellect because he could not afford the luxury of living in a library. Things had to be thought out for himself, slowly, painfully, with infinite groping. His failing, in William James' concept that any virtue carried too far may become a vice, was that of a too objective intelligence, a practical hard-headedness that eventually caused him to reject the ethical and normative inclinations of his youth in favor of the ruthless realism that found expression in the *Disquisition On Government*.

He was not an humble man, for humility has not yet been discovered as part of the Scotch-Irish Presbyterian temper, and in his later years he came to believe he had no limitations. In 1845, when old age and illness was upon him, he wrote, "In looking back, I see nothing to regret and little to correct."

Limitations, like every man, he naturally had. Yet almost instinctively he stayed within their area. No flights of the imagination, no adornment, no flourishes. His thought, like his speech, was terse and crowded, hard to grasp, harder to hold. Deadly serious, insisting upon absolute attention, his conversation was most generally apt to take the form of a kind of autocratic monologue.

"I have no desire to meet him again," a dinner companion

once remarked of him. "I hate a man who makes me think so much."

III

Since the measure of our interest in Calhoun is primarily the measure of his influence upon John Applegate, the lesser events of his political career are easily dismissed. It is enough to say that when he became Vice-President in 1832, after seven and one-half years as Secretary of War in President James Monroe's Cabinet, he had gained sufficiently in stature and reputation to have reasonable cause to expect to succeed Jackson as President. As was the case with his noted contemporaries, Daniel Webster and Henry Clay, the prospect of the Presidency haunted and tantalized him. His disclaimer of any such ambition may be discounted for what it is worth—the protest of one who protests too much.

Yet, while doing so, it has to be emphasized that no conscious motives influenced him except the highest. He had more than his share of vanity, liking to feel that he carried his state in his pocket like a rotten borough and that "when Calhoun took snuff, South Carolina sneezed," but he came to his conviction that he was the best man to govern the country more by the processes of thought than the workings of emotion. Nowhere are his complex and involved motives more clearly revealed than in those letters where he tries to explore his own state of mind.

"If the country wants an individual to carry on the sectional conflicts," he wrote in 1831, "I am not their man. I would not advance myself by sacrificing its true interests; but if they look to the higher considerations of peace, harmony and liberty, it would be the proudest incident of my life to be instrumental in promoting these great objects."

And in 1837: "So far from overestimating, I have no doubt that the very services which ought to recommend me to the country, and the qualities which ought to give confidence, constitute insuperable objections to my election. Nothing can raise me short of saving the country from convulsions."

Vanity is here, the largest kind of vanity, but it is a vanity that commands attention. John Calhoun had his petty moments but he was not a petty man. He had come to his conclusions, he had groped his way through to what he considered cardinal principles, and from those principles he would not yield. Writing to Robert Barnwell Rhett, later to become one of the foremost "fire-eaters" of South Carolina, he said:

"It seems to me that our true course is to occupy the old and independent ground on which we have stood for so many years, holding our principles and policies above the Presidential election."

What hopes he had for the future, what dreams of position or power, it is impossible to say. But he knew even then, watching the boil of slavery come to a head, that he was setting himself against the gathering forces of history——that the ever-increasing power of the industrial North, which had as its corollary an increased centralization of authority in the federal government, would not forever be denied. James Russell Lowell wrote of him in the *Biglow Papers:* "Mr. Calhoun has somehow acquired the name of a great statesman and, if it be great statesmanship to put lance in rest and run a tilt at the Spirit of the Age, with the certainy of being next moment hurled neck and heels into the dust amid universal laughter, he deserves the title."

It is doubtful, however, if Calhoun needed this monitorizing. Time after time he recorded his own awareness that his name and reputation might go down to ruin; yet, his autocratic temper only strengthened by opposition, he would not yield his ground. There was still the bounden duty of speaking what he saw in the only language he knew. And in all those crowded years, in all the swollen passages of debate, there was no one capable of truly answering him: so much is evident from the congressional records of the time. Not until Lincoln was a spokesman to appear capable of framing a reply, answering from first principles an argument based on first principles. Such an answer Calhoun might have understood. No other.

It makes an interesting and dramatic design to say that Calhoun might have been President, and the shape of history somehow changed, if he had not married a Charleston lady who would not receive a former barmaid into her drawing-room. Born Peggy O'Neal, now Mrs. Eaton, the barmaid was the wife of Jackson's Secretary of War. "She is as chaste as a virgin!" Old Hickory cried out in a Cabinet meeting, yielding generously to his habit of overstatement in what was probably the only such session ever given over to the consideration of a lady's virtue. Mrs. Calhoun, however, preferred to think otherwise. As high-handed as her husband was high-minded (tradition says she often locked him out of the house) she publicly snubbed Mrs. Eaton and refused to admit her to her home.

The testy Jackson, his love of direct action blocked by considerations of gallantry, vented his hostility upon Calhoun. Nor was his anger diminished when he learned that his Vice-President, instead of approving his breach of conduct in 1818 when he crossed into Florida and waged war against the Spaniards upon his own authority, as he had been led to believe, had instead been severely critical. The breach rapidly widened and soon the two men did not even try to conceal their hatred. Calhoun's presidential prospects grew increasingly slim and Jackson, upon retiring in 1837 to his Tennessee plantation, *The Hermitage*, said he harbored but one regret

——that he had not had the chance "either to hang Calhoun or shoot Clay."

The tone of Calhoun's thought, from this time onward, becomes more pronouncedly sectional in emphasis. It is now the South, rather than the nation, that claims his chief energy and attention. Because of this it has been deduced, perhaps too easily, that he lent himself to the ambitions of the Southern plantation imperialists out of bitterness and frustration. The bitterness and frustration cannot be denied, for he wanted the Presidency as much as he permitted himself to want anything, but if convenience demands a date be fixed for the turning point in his career, the year 1828 is better chosen.

The tariff act of 1828, called in South Carolina the "Tariff of Abominations," provided the immediate cause for a long-threatened period of governmental debate: capitalistic federalism and democratic liberalism were both under fire. How long Calhoun had been pondering the constitutional question we do not know; probably since his first year in Congress, certainly all during his term of office as Vice-President. In any case, confronted with the fact that the South was doomed to become a minority voice in the affairs of government, and that its whole social and economic structure was in danger, he set himself to find a constitutional defense for its threatened interests——hence the doctrines of nullification and States' Rights.

The attempt to do Calhoun justice need not involve any of that elaborate evasion called apology. He himself recognized and admitted his sectional and economic bias. Not only was he a member of the Southern ruling class, with the slaves and acres of his Fort Hill plantation to frame his position, but he was also the ruling class's outstanding spokesman. Yet if this much of his word is accepted, that the bias of his political philosophy derived from sectional and economic partisanship, there is an obligation to accept the rest of it——that, along with his desire to save the South, he also hoped to preserve the Union. It may be said he wished to do this on his own terms, which is true, and characteristic of him, but to see him as a conspirator plotting the destruction of his country solely to benefit the Southern *élite* is totally to misread his character.

"In speaking of abolition," he wrote in 1838 from Washington in a letter studded with typical misspellings, "you say it is better to part peacably at once, than to live in the state of indecision we do. That is a natural and common conclusion, but those who make it up do not think of the difficulty involved in the word; how many bleeding pours [pores] must be taken up in passing the knife of separation through a body politick, in order to make two of one, which has been so long bound together by so many ties, political, social and commercial. We must act throughout on the defensive, resorting to every probable means of arresting the evil, and only act, when all has been done, that can be, and when we shall be justified before God and man in taking the final step. Any other course would fail in its object."

Calhoun the conspirator is a mythical figure. Had the cause of States' Rights not been wedded to the cause of slavery, his position might have been more clearly understood. Like Jefferson, from whom he drew the States' Rights doctrine, he feared the drift toward federal centralization: equally, however, he came to distrust government based merely upon numerical majorities—rejecting, in the end, Jefferson's cardinal principle of democracy and coming to the position he describes and defends in the *Disquisition On Government*.

This book, one of the landmarks of American political theory, has a certain tragedy of its own. One of the most brilliant feats of the American intellect, containing perhaps the finest defense of minority rights ever written, it is like a majestic but nonetheless faulty dam trying to hold back the flood-waters of every current of democratic thought and aspiration.

Like Calhoun's career, the *Disquisition* is linked inseparably with slavery——to justify slavery is its major concern. But if this be kept constantly in mind, its incidental arguments and critique of government are still of considerable value. The ultimate test of any society, Calhoun held, was the measure of protection it provided for its weakest citizen. There was no guarantee that even the most democratic government would not degenerate into despotism should power come to be centralized in a few hands. There was always "the never-ending audacity of elected persons," the tax power was not immune to partiality, only the strictest scrutiny of a government's conduct could keep it honest and just. It therefore befell the political philosopher, he reasoned, to remember that no matter how carefully authority was distributed between the executive, legislative and judicial branches of the government, an ambitious majority, controlling all three branches, would still be able to deny the rights and the interests of the minority. The theory of the static state as held by the Federalists of the Montesquieu school, resulting from powers held in exact equilibrium, had in Calhoun's opinion been proved as much a failure as the belief of the Jeffersonians that a numerical majority would necessarily forward the cause of political justice.

To correct these two "miscalculations," Calhoun proposed the addition of another check upon federal authority——the veto power of the individual state upon an act of the national government. Such a veto power he held essential to constitutional government: "a power on the part of the ruled to prevent rulers from abusing their authority."

Beyond this, however, there lay a higher power: "a power to compel the parts of society to be just to one another, by compelling them to consult the interest of each other . . . by requiring the concurring assent of all the great and distinct interests of the community to the measures of the Government." Having thus come upon the doctrine of a concurrent majority, implicit to which was the concept of proportional representation——his most revolutionary idea—— Calhoun solved his problem by setting the will of a sectional or geographical majority above the will of the numerical majority. The lines of the *Disquisition* where he states his position may seem deadly dull, but they trace the lines of the Civil War.

> There are two different modes in which the sense of the community may be taken: one, simply by the right of suffrage, unaided; the other, by the right through a proper organism. Each collects the sense of the majority. But one regards numbers only, and considers the whole community one unit, having but one common interest throughout. The other [considers] the community as made up of different and conflicting interests . . . and takes the sense of each . . . and the united sense of all . . . as the sense of the entire community.

The validity of Calhoun's view is still a matter of debate, its correctness indicated by the "different and conflicting" interests that operate as an extra-legal part of government in the form of blocs and pressure groups, (but with no consideration of the sense of the entire community) its incorrectness manifest in the tragic experience of the Civil War. But clearly the young disciple of Thomas Jefferson who locked horns with Timothy Dwight had gone a long way in his political thinking. Subjecting the philosophy of his master to realistic analysis, pointing out what he took to be its cardinal error, he jettisoned some of its most cherished doctrines and left its fabric in shreds and tatters. To the faith of Jefferson he made this answer:

> It is a great and dangerous error to suppose that all people are equally entitled to liberty. It is a reward to be earned, not a blessing to be gratuitously lavished on all alike;——a reward reserved for the intelligent, the patri-

otic, the virtuous and deserving;——and not a boon to be bestowed on a people too ignorant to be capable either of appreciating or enjoying it. Nor is it any disparagement to liberty, that such is, and ought to be the case . . .

There is another error, not less great and dangerous, usually associated with the one which has just been considered. I refer to the opinion, that liberty and equality are so intimately united, that liberty cannot be perfect without perfect equality . . . To make equality of *condition* essential to liberty, would be to destroy both liberty and progress. It is indeed this inequality of condition between the front and rear ranks, in the march of progress, which gives so strong an impulse to the former to maintain their position, and to the latter to press forward into their files. This gives to progress its greatest impulse. To force the front rank back to the rear, or attempt to push forward the rear into line with the front, by the interposition of the government, would put an end to the impulse, and effectually arrest the march of progress.

This foundation having been laid, the conclusion was inevitable.

These great and dangerous errors have their origin in the prevalent opinion that all men are born free and equal;——than which nothing can be more unfounded and false. It rests upon the assumption of a fact, which is contrary to universal observation, in whatever light it may be regarded. It is, indeed, difficult to explain how an opinion so destitute of all sound reason, ever could have been so extensively entertained, unless we regard it as being confounded with another. I refer to the assertion that all men are equal in the state of nature; meaning, by a state of nature, a state of individuality, supposed to have existed prior to the social and political state . . . But such a state is purely hypothetical. It never did, nor can exist. It is, therefore, a great misnomer to call it *the state of nature*. Instead of being the natural state of man, it is, of all conceivable states, the most opposed to his nature——most repugnant to his feelings, and most incompatible with his wants. His natural state is, the social and political——the only one for which his Creater made him, and the only one in which he can preserve and perfect his race. As, then, there never was such a state as the so-called state of nature, if follows that men, instead of being born in it, are born in the social and political state; and of course, instead of being born free and equal, are born subject to the laws and institutions of the country where born, and under whose protection they draw their first breath.

It is here, in these central passages of the *Disquisition On Government*, that the thought of John Calhoun directly impinges upon the thought of John Applegate. Consider the latter's dilemma. The Declaration of Independence tells him, as a self-evident truth, that all men are created equal. Yet, on every side, every hour of the day, he sees a contrary stream of evidence. *A* is healthy, wealthy and wise while *B*, who lives just around the corner, is chronically ill, a ward of the town, and mentally inferior to a seven-year-old child. The *A*'s and *B*'s pass in endless file, flowing across his field of observation like protozoa across the field of a microscope. Is the self-evident then contrary to all observational evidence? Again there is a conflict, a tugging at cross-purposes, the awareness of a dilemma. As an American John Applegate has a complicated genealogy, but in this uncertainty he is as much a child of John Calhoun as of Thomas Jefferson. Common sense or idealism——how shall he choose?

For John Calhoun there was no such question. He, too, had looked at the observational evidence, harder than ever has John Applegate, and he was far too honest a realist to think in terms of leanings, emotions or sentiments. For him to go beyond his natural reach, and see all men as equal because of their equal communion in the mystery of the human species, would have been impossible. There may be deduced from this, as from his general indifference to all that lay beyond the harshly practical sphere, a certain unawareness of the moral world that indicates an incapacity for education. And it is such incapacity for education that condemns us all, in the region of sense, to substitute our idea of things for what things may be in themselves. So it was with Calhoun. Arrogantly confident of his own infallibility, idealizing slavery as one of the essential conditions of his larger idealism, the Greek republic, he substituted his idea of society for what society might be in itself. It was this that kept him incorrigibly pursuing what he called the "good"——the way of life, that is, that would most nearly satisfy the demands of his nature——regardless of its moral flaws and imperfections.

But the real clue to Calhoun's thought and character lies in the log college where he spent the most formative years of his life. The center of Puritanism, by the time of the Revolution, was beginning to shift to the Presbyterian South. Having died down somewhat in Cotton Mather's Boston, the fires of hell burned with all their original fury in Calhoun's South Carolina. The primitive Presbyterianism he absorbed in his youth was no less weighted with Calvinistic dogma than the creed of the New England fathers, coloring all his subsequent thought and human relations down to the day of his death in 1850 when he refused to summon his wife to his bedside lest she be put to an inconvenience.

"I hold," he wrote, "the duties of life to be greater than life itself, and that in performing them, even against hope, our labor is not lost. I regard this life very much as a struggle against evil, and that to him who acts on proper principle, the reward is in the struggle more than in victory itself."

Economic and sectional bias played a major part in bringing him to his rejection of democracy, but, beyond bias, how could he believe, this grim son of Calvin, that all men were equal and capable of self-government? He had known no such education as had Jefferson: he had gone to school to no liberal French and English philosophers: no happy winds of humanistic doctrine had played across his mind. If only his range of experience had been wider, one thinks; if only his incapacity for moral education had been less limited——what splendid feats of the intellect he might have performed.

All his life, however, save for the brief period spent in New England where his Calvinistic emphasis was merely further confirmed, he shuttled endlessly between the narrow provincialisms of South Carolina and Washington. How then can he be expected to come to Jefferson's humanism? Man innately good? He brushed aside that piece of tender-minded sentiment with a disdainful sweep of his hand. For the nature of man was not good, it was evil——such was the spiritual lesson of the log college of his youth. And this being so, the evil that is man, how could he be believed capable of governing himself in any way but evilly? It then followed, inevitably, that the elect, not the people, had the right to rule. To rule and have slaves.

"Let me not be understood as admitting, even by implication, that the existing relations between the two races in the slaveholding states is an evil," Calhoun cried out in a speech delivered in the Senate in 1837. "I take higher ground! I hold that it is, instead of an evil, a good——a positive good!"

Again, throughout the crowded passages of this oration, he makes us realize how fully he anticipated all the spokesmen of feudalism in our time. And, with equal clarity, we are also made to realize that we have come but one step beyond John Cotton asking: "If the people be governors, who shall be governed?" and answering, "As for monarchy and aristocracy, they are both of them clearly approved, and directed in Scripture." To find slavery good, a positive good, is merely to take the next step in a logical progression and introduce the doctrine of theocratic New England into a new and harsher frame.

It is also, in human terms, to complete the tragedy. The inheritor of Jefferson's mantle becomes the impassioned defender of man's right to enslave man. The political philosopher looking at the face of society, finds there, in a kind of monstrous narcissism, only a mirror intended to reflect the will and image of John Calhoun.

"Whether it be too great confidence in my own ability," he is quoted as saying, "I cannot say; but what I think I see, I see with so much apparent clearness as not to leave me a choice to pursue any other course, which has always given me the impression that I acted with the force of destiny."

This is like a scythe cutting down the last grasses of our sympathy. He ends by giving us only his wasted genius to regret. We must not think, however, that he would be concerned by this. He held the struggle important, not the victory, and he would be content with his reward. Thomas Jefferson lies at rest in a small plot on the slopes of Monticello. The whole South is the grave of John Calhoun.

· 4 ·

LET US KNEEL TO GOOD
ABE LINCOLN

The American As Patron Saint

IT IS John Applegate's habit, every summer evening when
the weather is fine, to leave the house and walk to the
edge of town. It is not far, only a few minutes stroll,
and when he gets to the open country he climbs a little
wooded hill that rises against the stars. Standing on its crest,
the lights of the town shining in the darkness behind him, he
looks into the night. Most of the time his mind dwells on
little things, the small problems of family and business, but
there are occasional moments when the ordinary world slips
away and he is conscious of the vast immensity that is
America. He knows as well as anyone that the airplane has
bridged the oceans, that in one day he can travel by automobile twice as far as his father traveled by covered wagon in
two months, but John Applegate, divorced as he is from the
compulsions of the seasons, planting no seed and reaping no
harvest, is still a creature of the earth. A mile is a mile: the
geographical vastness of America remains unchanged.

He feels, generally, a pride in this largeness. Having had
the excellence of work, enterprise and success dinned into
his ears since childhood, he has a respect and admiration for
bigness——big buildings, big fortunes, big ventures. Anything less than Niagara is not truly a waterfall: anything less
than a continent is not quite a country.

European visitors, coming to the United States, are invariably troubled by this reverence for bigness. Either they are frightened by what endears America to many Americans—its complexity, its plurality, its diverseness—or, like André Siegfried, they see the potentiality of America, inherent in its vastness, frustrated by a dreary social pragmatism they hold to be the "religion" of modern America. Nor is it difficult for these critics to summon a weight of evidence to support their points of view. The standardization they deplore, the materialism, the emphasis upon conformity—all are here. It is also true, as other foreign appraisers have noticed, that John Applegate, unlike the average European, has no sense of fate or destiny. No arch of mystery, or of terror, bends across his sky. The world, he feels, is a safe and relatively comfortable place, watched over by a sympathetic God who demands only that his children be cheerful and optimistic and trust wholly in the future.

As good a Christian as the next man, and a deacon of his church, John Applegate's idea of religion is apt to be confused with his idea of worldly success. A Christian man, by Calvinistic and Puritan definition, is a prosperous man: to be prosperous, and irreligious, is to John Applegate somehow unthinkable—that is why, to the extreme irritation of his critics on the left, he has never been able to convince himself that the robber-baron capitalists were truly immoral or wicked men: the mark of the Lord's favor was too clearly upon them. Religion, then, while necessary, must not be carried too far. Sufficient unto the Sabbath is the church-going thereof. For the other six days of the week, a sensible man will put his attention to the practical business of making a living and not burden his mind with considerations of the moral universe—the physical one we live in is difficult and complicated enough.

Such crudity of thought, however, much as it lends itself to ridicule and satire, does not absolve John Applegate from moments of spiritual hunger. These are rare moments indeed, for he is not a man given either to metaphysical speculation or spiritual retreat, but when they come he is troubled by a vague sense of loneliness, some hint of man's solitary inconsequence in the immense eternity of space and time. The emotion that falls upon him, swiftly coming and swiftly gone, is much the same emotion that caused Henry Adams to write, in *Mont-Saint-Michel*, "Man is an imperceptible atom always trying to become one with God." John Applegate, no less than Adams, feels the need for a larger, deeper, more encompassing identification: the individual would be fused into something more enduring than himself.

To tell John Applegate that such moments are moments of spiritual necessity, to say that in him there is some residue of religious aspiration left unsatisfied by the ambiguities of moral materialism——this would bring another look of puzzlement to his face. Lacking a sense of mystery, never greatly troubled by either the fear or love of God, he likewise lacks the knowledge that the religious impulse may exist independently of church or temple, and that, if blocked in one direction, it must inevitably seek escape in another. He would be as hard put to understand this, (so fixed and determined is his understanding of religion) as he would be to comprehend that his reverence for Abraham Lincoln——the American above all others who has a vivid existence in his mind——may also be regarded as a religious manifestation. While it would be an exaggeration to say that Lincoln is as valuable symbolically to John Applegate as was the Virgin to the devout of the Twelfth Century, it may yet be said that, in a singularly thin moral climate, he is the American patron saint. Indeed, had he not existed, as Voltaire is reported to have remarked of God, it would have been necessary to invent him. Man does not live by bread alone and even a people largely indifferent to spiritual matters must have a vessel to contain the highest aspirations of their hope and faith.

That this should be so, that John Applegate should find meaning and inspiration in the memory of Lincoln whenever the nation is shadowed by trouble or disaster, is on first consideration one of the strangest circumstances of American life. Of all the great Americans to whom he might pledge his spiritual allegiance, and by that allegiance lift to the position of what anthropologists might call the father-spirit of the tribe, Lincoln is the one man whose life and character most violates those copy-book maxims which lie at the core of the genteel tradition John Applegate has never paused either to question or deny——a tradition, it is understood, that depends more upon Mrs. Applegate than upon her husband.

Consider, for instance, the mystery surrounding the facts of Lincoln's birth. That he was illegitimate, (though not, as folklore would have it, the natural son of either Henry Clay or John Calhoun) is well within the area of probability. That his mother was likewise illegitimate was a belief he himself held; his law-partner and biographer, William H. Herndon, telling us that he believed any such ability as he might have came to him as an inheritance from his mother through her mysterious father, "a Virginia aristocrat."

An illegitimate son of an illegitimate mother: what, ordinarily, would John Applegate say to this? Could his moral code be more deeply offended? And should it not be equally offended, in view of his admiration for energy and enterprise, by the fact that Lincoln was what he would call "shiftless" ——one who in his youth, according to John Hanks, was not much good at any kind of work but dreaming; and who, in later life, so Dennis Hanks tells us, "was lazy——a very lazy man."

Lincoln, furthermore, spent many years of his life chronically in debt——due to circumstances beyond his control, it is true, but nonetheless, in John Applegate's vocabulary of censure, "a man who couldn't pay his bills." In appearance he was more striking than prepossessing, altogether indifferent to the impression he made on others, frequently sweaty under the armpits, always needing a hair cut. ("Here's your Old Abe," newsboys cried out when he became the Presidential nominee in 1860. "He'll look better when he gets his hair combed.") Suppose a stranger answering this description should walk into John Applegate's drugstore: would he not be tempted to remark upon the virtues of cleanliness and the value of a good appearance?

And what of Ann Rutledge: what of Mary Todd? Presuming it possible for John Applegate to overlook Lincoln's lesser shortcomings, how is it possible for him to ignore the affront given to the institution he respects above all others? Here was a man who, married to one woman, is said to have dreamed and brooded on another; who went to his wedding believing he was going "to Hell, I reckon," and, in all truth, did. Is this the sort of person John Applegate is prepared to revere? The more we inquire, the deeper the mystery becomes——a mystery, however, more apparent than real.

It is most readily explained in terms of legend and myth. If John Applegate does not like to see his heroes painted "warts and all," neither do most of his countrymen. After it was apparent that Lincoln could not be denied the central position in the hierarchy of great Americans——not by slander nor ridicule, contumely nor vilification——only one course remained open: he must be made fit for polite society.

While Emily Applegate, belonging to a younger and more forthright generation, is willing to accept the likelihood of Nancy Hanks' illegitimacy as "one of those things," her father finds it more comforting to believe that she actually had the coat-of-arms that is sometimes claimed for her, and that she grew up in Cavalier Virginia "hunting, hawking, and fishing in the great estates of nearly a thousand acres." Nor does he find it any less comforting to believe that instead of being illiterate, as was probably the case, she had enough learning to teach her son how to read and write, and spent her evenings giving him moral instruction from the pages of the Bible.

It is not to be imagined from this, however, that John Applegate looks down upon the poverty Lincoln was born into. The more humbly a man starts out, the higher he can rise. All he asks of poverty is that it be worthy; that those who live in it do so with a decent consideration of the middle-class verities. He likes to think, therefore, that Lincoln was never late to school, never rude, noted for keeping his clothes clean. And if it pleases him to believe that Lincoln likewise never drank or swore, and never chewed tobacco, he finds it even more pleasing to look upon the rail-splitter as a "self-made man." Lincoln, he might say, justified his poverty by growing out of it.

As for Ann Rutledge and Mary Todd, here he escapes the dilemma by refusing to confront it. He has some dim comprehension that Mary Todd was a difficult person to get along with——(wasn't there something about her driving old Abe from the house without any supper?)——but it is Ann Rutledge who is wedded to Lincoln in his mind. The agony caused by the death of a young sweetheart, and passion ennobled by loss, is one of man's oldest and most cherished tales, while the day-by-day torment of living with a shrewish, ambitious woman who was eventually to grow mad is too grimly tragic ever to find acceptance by an imagination—— national as well as personal——that demands primarily of love that it go to the altar in the last chapter and live happily ever after.

That a cloud of doubt hangs over the romance, that there

is not the slightest scrap of reliable evidence touching upon it, matters as little to John Applegate as it mattered to Edgar Lee Masters when he wrote in the *Spoon River Anthology:*

> I am Ann Rutledge who sleep beneath these weeds,
> Beloved in life of Abraham Lincoln,
> Wedded to him, not through union,
> But through separation.
> Bloom forever, O Republic,
> From the dust of my bosom!

Mary Todd lends herself to no such celebration. Long since held unworthy of Lincoln, unfit for his place and destiny, she has been largely forgotten. Nor does the fact that more meaning and illumination is to be found in the somber passage of Lincoln's marriage than in his doubtful romance with Ann Rutledge make any difference——John Applegate still prefers to pass it over in silence.

In all this, however, there is an element of unfairness. John Applegate has been made too much a pawn in an intellectual game. While it is true that the Lincoln of his imagination is largely a Lincoln of myth, and that this myth has been shaped to conform to the measurements of respectability, it is no less true that his reverence of Lincoln implies at least a partial rejection of those polite standards and values to which he generally adheres. One of the most revealing characteristics of John Applegate, generally overlooked, is that while he himself never strays from the path of propriety, his favorite people in American history are most likely to be men who have——Daniel Boone, Davy Crockett, Sam Houston, Andrew Jackson, Lincoln above them all. Whether or not this is a form of escape, an obscure release from certain restraints and conformities that weigh more heavily upon him than perhaps he himself imagines——these considerations need not occupy us now. Certain it is, however, that the gaunt six-foot-four figure of Lincoln, gnarled and bearded and worn by toil, is closer to him than the sternly excellent George Washington, or Thomas Jefferson, pacing the corridors of his admirable mind.

A scholar in search of a thesis might deduce from this, along with other evidence, that John Applegate is still a pioneer at heart——or, if not that, that his imagination is most excited by those figures of history and legend who manage to return to him some of the excitement that gripped his fathers when their wagons creaked across the plains of promise toward the future's dawn. Such a thesis, like most, would probably end by proving little because it tries to prove too much; yet, granting our imaginary scholar his right to speculate, we might see him recording, possibly as a footnote, that John Applegate would be likely to name Zane Grey as his favorite author, and Gary Cooper, the frontiersman in store-bought clothes, his favorite movie star.

The emancipated modern, having little patience with John Applegate to begin with, would look upon these preferences merely as further evidence of his shallowness of mind and badness of taste. And Sonny Applegate's two favorite literary characters, Superman and Tarzan of the Apes, would be regarded as being similarly unfortunate. But these heroes of young America, if their appeal may be so arbitrarily limited, embody all the characteristics of the frontiersman——his imagination, his fearlessness, his ability to win through no matter what the odds——and their amazing feats are constantly suggestive of the fabulous exploits of Paul Bunyan and Mike Fink. No matter what the strength or cunning of their enemies, the latter are invariably compelled to admit their defeat and say, like the treed 'coon in the Davy Crockett story, "Don't shoot, Mister——I'll come down." Tarzan is the frontiersman returned to the jungle: Superman the plainsman projected into the future.

Our imaginary scholar might also urge us to consider those

occupations that have most excited the American mind; to examine the progression that runs from pioneer to pony-rider to steamboat captain to railroad engineer to airplane pilot. In every instance the native esteem for the pathfinder comes through, no matter what the field. Thus, while we may find fault with the statement that John Applegate is a pioneer at heart, we may well believe that at least part of his admiration for Lincoln derives from those elements in the latter's character suggestive of the frontier.

It is here better, perhaps, to say affection rather than admiration——Lincoln is liked as well as loved: his humor alone would have been enough to make him John Applegate's favorite American. The national habit of story-telling——the tale told for its own sake, as moral adornment, as part of conversation——this habit reached its high climax in the stories of Lincoln. A latterday America, grown more sophisticated in its tastes, might find these stories tedious and dull; corny, Emily Applegate would call them. Yet, as Miss Constance Rourke was the first to notice, they draw together the memories and fantasies of a whole region——more than one region ——and yield a hardy comic poetry that is part of our popular lore.

Lincoln's humor was the humor of the frontier, rough as a chestnut-burr and broad as the blade of a logger's axe. Before he was twenty he floated down the Mississippi to New Orleans on a raft; one of his first law cases arose from the opposition of the flatboatmen to a projected bridge across the Mississippi. By the time he came to manhood the riverman's lore and vocabulary were as familiar to him as the speech and fables of Kentucky and Illinois. He knew the tall tales about Mike Fink——the boatmen's hero who rode a wild moose and drowned a she-wolf with his hands——as well as those centering about Davy Crockett, just then coming into his legendary fame. No less familiar to him, according to Carl

Sandburg, were the stories in *Joe Miller's Jests*, a slap-happy compendium of tales and anecdotes ranging from English puns and Irish bulls to Jewish folklore. All this and more went into his story-telling; he used the whole American strain. Mimicry, caricature, ridicule, burlesque——each was within his range. His was a hardy school of humor, horny-handed and contentious, though his most telling shafts were often delivered with an elaborately innocent air, as in his famous ridicule of Douglas' fondness for drink.

"I was not aware until now that Mr. Douglas' father was a cooper," he said on one occasion. "I am certain he was a very good one, for"——and now he bowed to Douglas——"he has made one of the best whiskey casks I have ever seen."

Some of the stories he is known to have told are still being told today; John Applegate has heard them in his drugstore. And behind all of them, as behind the man himself, there lay a large background of backwoods experience. The whole psychology of horse-trading, for example, is traced in his story about the boy who was showing a horse at a Kentucky fair.

"Look here, boy," a man said. "Ain't that horse got the splints?"

"Mister," the boy answered. "I don't know what the splints is, but if it's good for him, he's got it; if it ain't good for him, he ain't got it."

"A walking, stalking library of stories," Carl Sandburg calls him. They came from anywhere and everywhere; his memory held them like a sponge. ("I am only a retail dealer," he said.) Many of them had a Biblical basis, like the one about the schoolboy who tripped over the names of Shadrach, Meshach, and Abednego, and set up a wail as his turn to recite came round once more——"Look there, marster—— there comes them same damn three fellers again!" There were others in which the Negro figured, revolving about his simple approach to religion and the way he humanized the characters in the Bible. Lincoln told of a carnival balloonist going up in New Orleans, sailing for hours, and finally coming down over a cotton-field. The gang of Negroes picking cotton saw a man floating from the sky in a blue-silk chariot, in silver spangles, wearing golden slippers. They fled, thinking the Day of Judgment had surely come——all but one old fellow so crippled with rheumatism he could not get away. He waited until the balloonist hit the earth and walked toward him. Then he mumbled: "Howdy, Massa Jesus. How's yo pa?"

Nor was Lincoln above turning his laughter against himself. When asked by one of his Springfield neighbors how it felt to be President, he said: "You know about the man who was tarred and feathered and ridden out of town on a rail, don't you? A man in the crowd asked him how he was enjoying it, and his reply was that if it wasn't for the honor of the thing, he'd much rather walk." He also liked to tell about a hard-bitten old Democrat who came up to him and said, after a time of preliminary glaring: "They tell me you're a self-made man——well, if you are, all I've got to say is that you did a damned bad job of it."

There may be detected in Lincoln's humor, as Miss Rourke has said, a synthesis of two of the more pronounced strains of native comedy. He showed the backwoods ebullience, calling a bowie-knife a scythe and telling of the brawl in which a man fought himself out of one coat and into another, but, along with this, there was an economy of speech that seems to have been derived from the New England strain which was part of his ancestry, doubtless sharpened by many encounters with the Yankee traders who went West. In a speech made in protest against the Mexican War he told of an Illinois farmer who protested, "I ain't greedy about land. I only want what jines mine." The laconic statement is

Yankee, (suggesting the famous Calvin Coolidge story in which the Boom Age president, pressed by his wife to repeat what had been said by a minister on the broad subject of sin, is made to reply, "He's agin it.") but the hidden inflation, the implicit background, belong entirely to the West.

How much influence the Bible had upon Lincoln's speech is hard to determine. Such traces of it as we are able to find, however, as in the Douglas debate where he says, "This argument of the judge is the same old serpent that says, 'You work and I eat, you toil and I will enjoy the fruits of it,'" have all been reshaped and altered by frontier experience. His images and metaphors were as unmistakably American as his face: "It will grow hair on a pumpkin"; "slick as a blacksnake out of its skin"; "there are too many hogs [political hangers-on] for the tits." There was the stuff of poetry in his speech——earthy, plain and homespun, coming out of the life he led and the life led all around him——and often we see the artist at work. But despite all the praise given the stories he told, and to the Gettysburg address, it still may be wondered why he has been so infrequently recognized as one of the major American writers, denied the place that is rightfully his.

In saying it was Lincoln, rather than Mark Twain, who first made use of the firm native idiom that is held to be the latter's great contribution to American style, there is no intent to deny Mark Twain's largeness of stature. One cannot read Lincoln, however, without being struck that it was he, no less than Mark Twain, who did for the American language what Dante, in another time and place, did for the Italian——making it, that is, a medium of major expression. The Douglas debates are as great a landmark in our literature as in our politics. The various characteristics that distinguish Mark Twain's style——its firmness, its ease, its flavor——are likewise present in Lincoln's.

I do not rise to speak now, if I can stipulate with the audience to meet me here at half-past six or seven o'clock. It is now past five, and Judge Douglas has spoken over three hours. It will take me as long as it has taken him. That will carry us beyond eight o'clock at night. Now, every one of you who can remain that long can just as well get his supper, meet me at seven, and remain an hour or two later. The judge has already informed you that he is to have an hour to reply to me. I doubt not but you have been a little surprised to learn that I have consented to give one of his high reputation and known ability this advantage of me. Indeed, my consenting to it, though reluctant, was not wholly unselfish, for I suspected, if it were understood that the Judge was entirely done, you Democrats would leave and not hear me; but by giving him the close, I felt confident you would stay for the fun of hearing him skin me alive.*

It would be an understandable error if, Lincoln's authorship of this passage being unknown to us, we should credit it to Mark Twain. It has the same tone, the same grain and texture, the same shrewd knowledge of native psychology. It might be held, indeed, that Lincoln actually wrote the better prose––simpler, more direct, more ruggedly honest––and was capable of deeper emotional statement. What, in Mark Twain, is comparable to the Second Inaugural Address: or to the words spoken by Lincoln to his Springfield neighbors from the platform of the train that was waiting to take him to Washington after his first election?

No one, not in my situation, can appreciate my feeling of sadness at this parting. To this place, and the kindness of these people, I owe everything. Here I have lived a quarter of a century and have passed from a young to an old man. Here my children have been born, and one

---

* The opening remarks of a speech delivered on October 16, 1854, in Peoria, Ilinois––probably the first great speech of Lincoln's career.

is buried. I now leave, not knowing when or whether ever I may return, with a task before me greater than that which rested upon Washington. Without the assistance of the Divine Being who ever attended him, I cannot succeed. With that assistance, I cannot fail. Trusting in Him who can go with me, and remain with you, and be everywhere for good, let us confidently hope that all will yet be well. To His care commending you, as I hope in your prayers you will commend me, I bid you an affectionate farewell.

But now, the comparison between Twain and Lincoln having been made, it must be dismissed. A purely creative writer like Twain, given at once the freedom and the limitations of fiction, cannot be expected to speak, as did Lincoln, in terms of urgent personal immediacy. Much of the homage paid to Mark Twain, however, still more properly belongs to Lincoln. The room of our admiration is large enough, surely, to find a place for them both.

II

The influence of the frontier upon Lincoln's thought was no less marked than upon his speech and humor. A son of the same pioneer back-country that produced Thomas Jefferson and Andrew Jackson, endowed with the same spontaneous democracy, the Lincoln of reality has been so eclipsed by the Lincoln of myth that his most significant contribution to our political thought has been generally overlooked. His greatness here depends, not so much upon his ability as a social theorist, for in his large humanity he preferred fable to dialectic, as upon his contribution to the continuing American debate that revolves about the universal argument as to whether the many or the few have the right to rule.

In the way the assumptions of Cotton Mather and William Byrd of Westover were challenged by Thomas Jefferson, only then to be restated and buttressed with new arguments by John Calhoun——in this structure of affirmation and denial there can be detected a pattern of thrust and parry, charge and countercharge, that may be taken as the basic design of American history. That the Civil War was the most dramatic occasion in that design needs no further emphasis. Lincoln's association with the Civil War, basic to which was the issue of slavery, has given rise to the notion that the desire to abolish slavery was implicit in his every act. It was the preservation of the Union, however, rather than the abolition of slavery, that lay in the forefront of his purpose.

Having experienced violence at first hand, a certain measure of violence being present in every frontier society, Lincoln rejected it as a solution. In the First Inaugural he said he had "no lawful right" to ban the South's peculiar institution, and when the war broke out he quickly rebuked those Northern leaders who saw the conflict as directed primarily against slavery. He never gave the idea formal statement, for he seemed almost to shun theoretical speculation, but it is clear that he regarded the state——or, rather, the institution of government——as an arbiter between opposing groups with conflicting interests. Unlike the Hot-Heads on one side, and the Abolitionists on the other, he believed in a spirit of compromise and mutual concession.

This is plainly indicated by his remarks on the Missouri Compromise. "The Compromise," he said, "ought to be restored. We ought to elect a House of Representatives which will vote its restoration. If by any means we omit to do this, what follows? Slavery may or may not be established in Nebraska. But whether it be or not, we shall have repudiated ——discarded from the councils of the nation——the spirit of compromise . . . But restore the Compromise, and what then? We thereby restore the national faith, the national confidence, the national feeling of brotherhood. We thereby reinstate the spirit of concession and compromise, that spirit which has never failed us in past perils, and which may be safely trusted for all the future . . . It would be worth to the nation a hundred years' purchase of peace and prosperity."

His views on slavery underwent considerable modification, and he came to feel that an attempt was being made to place the institution on a new basis, "making it perpetual, national and universal," but not even in the Emancipation Proclamation did he suggest that its abolition was his major purpose. In an open letter to Horace Greeley he wrote: "My paramount object in this struggle is to save the Union. It is *not* to destroy slavery."

But the issue of slavery, transcending all others, could not be kept separate from the adjacent issue of democracy. The words of Jefferson's charter were part of the political and moral climate in those threatening years. The principles of the Declaration intruded themselves upon every man's thought and attention. Lincoln, like Calhoun before him, was forced to return to them and consider their meaning anew. Calhoun, subjecting the Declaration to the criticism of a ruthless realism, had tried to destroy it. Lincoln, coming from the same kind of society in which the idea of American democracy had been found, gave its principles new and compelling statement. When he again joined Douglas in debate in Springfield, Illinois, on July 17, 1858, a spokesman capable of framing a reply to Calhoun was as last found. Lincoln said:

> I adhere to the Declaration of Independence. If Judge Douglas and his friends are not willing to stand by it, let them come up and amend it . . . In his construction of the Declaration last year, Judge Douglas said it only meant that Americans in America were equal to Englishmen in England. Then, when I pointed out to him that by this rule he excludes the Germans, the Irish, the Portuguese, and all the other peoples who have come

among us since the Revolution, he reconstructs his construction. In his last speech he tells us it meant Europeans . . . I expect ere long he will introduce another amendment to his definition. But who shall say, "I am the superior, and you are the inferior?" . . . I have said that I do not understand the Declaration to mean that all men were created equal in all respects . . . but I suppose that it does mean to declare that all men are equal in some respects; that they are equal in their right to "life, liberty and the pursuit of happiness."

Lincoln, no less than Calhoun, had looked at the observational evidence. He knew, as well as the other, that it is the inequality of men, rather than their equality, that is subject to empirical confirmation. But unlike Calhoun, who discovered in such inequality his final argument for the inevitablity of the elect, and unlike Jefferson who rested his case too largely on sentiment, Lincoln faced the problem squarely (or was driven to face it, for he had to be prodded into intellectual effort) and sought to establish a working relationship between a moral principle on one hand, and, on the other, a fact of reality. As reluctant as Calhoun to go beyond the observational process, totally disinterested in trying to prove the unprovable, he cut across theory and dialectic and went to the heart of the matter, affirming man's right, whatever his individual condition, to his dignity and station as man. No proof is needed to establish this right, he correctly understood, because it exists itself as part of proof. Nor did he, like Jefferson, fall into the mistake of thinking it derived from some natural "law." In his Gettysburg Address he called it simply a proposition——using the word, it would seem, in its accepted metaphysical context: a matter, that is, of belief and faith. It was his simple genius to understand, more clearly than any of his contemporaries, that the ethical content of the Declaration of Independence is the moral cement that holds the American system together, and gives the idea of democracy more than a political importance.

Democracy, Lincoln felt, had a special mission and purpose. In this he suggests not only Emerson, Whitman and Thoreau, but also de Tocqueville who wrote that, instead of being a novel accident, democracy was the most ancient and permanent tendency to be found in history, and discovered in it certain religious implications.

> All men have aided it by their exertions: those who have intentionally labored in its cause, and those who have served it unwittingly; those who have fought for it and those who declared themselves its opponents, have all been driven along in the same track, have all labored to one end, some ignorantly and some willingly; all have been blind instruments in the hands of God. The gradual development of democracy is therefore a providential fact, and it possesses all the characteristics of a Divine decree: it is universal, it is durable, it constantly eludes all human interference, and all events as well as all men contribute to its progress. It has a nobility of its own.

To Lincoln, as to de Tocqueville, there was a moral purpose to democracy. It was not important as a way of organizing the affairs of society, or for its promise of a higher standard of living, but because of the spiritual and ethical illumination it contained.

"The principles of Jefferson," he wrote, "are the principles and axioms of a free society. And yet they are denied and evaded, with no small show of success. One dashingly calls them 'glittering generalities.' Another bluntly calls them 'self-evident lies.' And others insidiously argue that they apply to 'superior races.' These expressions, differing in form, are identical in object and effect——the supplanting of the principles of free government, and restoring those of classification, caste and legitimacy. They are the vanguard, the miners and sappers of returning despotism. We must repulse them, or they will subjugate us."

To call Lincoln a spiritual leader, and more particularly a prophet, may seem to be stretching definition to the breaking point. But prophecy, in its truest meaning, has for its concern not the future but the present; the function of the prophet, in Emerson's words, being "to cheer, to raise and to guide men by showing them facts amid appearances." The office of prophecy, in this understanding, as Van Wyck Brooks has said, is to reveal such facts as are obscured by appearances, to show that life is not being but becoming, to give moral and ethical example, to speak always in the belief that the great seed-bed of humanity contains always within itself the possibility of a spiritual awakening.

This possibility Lincoln never once doubted. The Gettysburg Address is a declaration of faith in that possibility. "The world," he said, "will little note nor long remember what we say here, but it can never forget what they did here. It is for us, the living, rather, to be dedicated here to the unfinished work which they who fought here have thus far so nobly advanced. It is rather for us to be here dedicated to the great task remaining before us——that from these honored dead we take increased devotion; that we here highly resolve that these dead shall not have died in vain; that this nation, under God, shall have a new birth of freedom; and that government of the people, by the people, for the people, shall not perish from the earth."

Those who rejected the Declaration of Independence, dismissing it as a collection of "glittering generalities" and "self-evident lies," would have found the Gettysburg Address similarly lacking in conviction. Nor was it highly regarded when Lincoln spoke on Cemetery Hill: he himself thought he had miserably failed. "The cheek of every American," said *The Chicago Times*, "must tingle with shame as he reads the silly, flat and dish-watery utterances of the man who has to be pointed out to intelligent foreigners as the President of the United States." But if we rise above such paltriness of consideration, struggling toward Lincoln's own moral plane, we may perhaps see it for what it truly is——an insistence upon facts amid appearances; a showing that life is not being but becoming; a call for a spiritual awakening; one of the greatest prophetic utterances, in short, ever spoken on the American continent.

That the age-old pattern of the Christ story——the humble birth, the long preparation, the martyr's death——should have been found in the drama of Lincoln's life is not surprising. That he should have come to be the American patron saint is less surprising still. Myth and folklore may be forgotten: so many the various American traditions Lincoln has come to represent. John Applegate would still turn to him in moments of necessity because he was the one great man among us whose life was ruled by love. For this alone he would be hallowed in our memory——the best we are, the best we can hope to be——and remain a symbol for all the world.

ANDREW CARNEGIE

OR FROM RAGS TO RICHES

The American As Success Story

WHEN THE Civil War broke out in 1861, and the Union armies were routed at the first battle of Manassas, there came to Washington as assistant in charge of the military railroads and telegraph division of the War Department, a young Scotch immigrant whose family had settled in Pittsburg. Occasionally, during those early months of war, Abraham Lincoln would come into the young man's office and sit on his desk, worried and anxious for information. The destiny that had brought the youth to this place of importance, at the age of twenty-six, would seem strange enough: the destiny that was later to lift him to the highest ranges of material success, and make his name everywhere synonymous with the possession of great wealth, would seem more than strange—almost incredible, threaded with accident and with chance, joined to the destiny of a continent.

John Applegate, however, to whom the young man's saga is not altogether unfamiliar, does not find it incredible. Howsoever amazing he may find some things, he finds nothing amazing in success. It is one of those things, like a high standard of living, he considers essential to America. Pyramids of wealth, like the pyramids of the New York skyline, are part of his national landscape. He would find it as hard to imagine an America bereft of millionaires as to think of Manhattan in terms of two-story dwellings. If there were no millionaires, he might say, a poor boy could not hope to be one.

Nor is this because, as has so often been charged, he is obsessed with a love of the almighty dollar; this is an easy and convenient view. He is material-minded, to be sure, and lives in a civilization materialistic to the core, but as for money itself, as George Santayana has written, he makes, loses, spends and gives it away with a very light heart. Driven by the mores of his culture into moral materialism, busy since boyhood with the traditional American business of getting ahead, he is wont to emphasize money because of its value and convenience as a measuring device. It is, indeed, almost the only one he knows. This is why, though he is fully to appreciate a good man, or a kind one, his deepest admiration is likely to be reserved for the one who has been successful—the one, that is, who has money in the bank: he has been measured in the scales and found not wanting.

Looking upon statistics as truth, convinced that figures do not lie, it is almost impossible for John Applegate not to be swayed by the size of a man's fortune. There is involved, ultimately, something of that American reverence of bigness we have already noticed. The historic American fortunes are almost entirely impersonal to him. He respects them, in the end, for the same reason he respects Niagara Falls. Cubic tons of water, cubic tons of wealth—both have the same impressiveness. And if the cubic tons of wealth should happen to take on a certain tangibility, as in the form of skyscrapers, college buildings or libraries, the impressiveness becomes all the more.

There is every reason, consequently, for Andrew Carnegie, the young telegrapher who gained the notice of Abraham Lincoln, to occupy a salient position in John Applegate's mind. He has been aware of the steel-master ever since he borrowed his first book from the public library; a circumstance Mark Twain clearly foresaw when he wrote, in one of the private papers Bernard De Voto has collected under the title *Mark Twain In Eruption*, "Carnegie has arranged that his name be famous in the mouths of men for centuries to come . . . I think that in three or four centuries Carnegie libraries will be considerably thicker in the world than churches."

It was Twain's belief, not free of cynicism, that Carnegie shrewdly set out to perpetuate his memory: "He has bought fame and paid cash for it." The motives behind the industrialist's philanthropy were actually more complicated, but Twain was correct in believing that Carnegie's memory was to be kept fresh and green by the libraries that bear his name. He has walked through their portals into American folklore. John Applegate thinks of him, whenever his name happens to be brought to mind, as a canny Scotch Aladdin with a magic steel lamp who spent his life making money in order to give the money away. Shrewd or not shrewd, Carnegie could not have arranged things more to his liking.

Plutarch is but another name in John Applegate's mind, put there during the high-school years that also gave to his memory the names of Julius Caesar, Henry VIII and Ivanhoe, but he would readily agree with the Greek historian's general precept that the purpose and justification of biography is to set up good examples—models of successful men. This being so, he could think of no better book to put into the hands of the young, for practical instruction and moral guidance, than Carnegie's *Autobiography;* a book which, as we read it in the twilight of the era he helped inaugurate, suggests the sort of confession an Horatio Alger hero might have written in his old age.

Our worthy protagonist is grizzled now, looking not unlike a pint-size General U.S. Grant in a pair of golf-knickers and a plaid cap, and, basking in the Indian summer of memory on the high plateau of success, he can look back upon the past and find it good. The way of life, which other men have found steep and tortuous in the extreme, seems in retrospect as sharply defined as the roadway of a railroad, pushing its way through the wilderness. One simply starts in the proper direction, keeps one's eye always on the main chance, and eventually one arrives at a castle in Scotland with the King of England himself coming for a visit——it is as simple and easy as that.

The story of Carnegie's life, however, was somewhat more complicated than his autobiography would have us believe. The son of a militant weaver whose father and brother were outstanding leaders of the early Scotch radical movement, the one being the publisher of what is sometimes called the first left-wing journal in Scotland and the other a Chartist and republican firebrand, Carnegie was born in Dumfermline, Scotland, on the 25th of November, 1835, in the attic of a one-story house. His family migrating to America to escape their grinding poverty, he went to work at the age of twelve as a bobbin-boy in a cotton-mill at a dollar and twenty cents a week. His father was employed in the same mill and, in his autobiography, Carnegie describes the long hours of winter toil that stretched from dark to dark.

> The hours hung heavily upon me and in the work itself I took but little pleasure; but the cloud had a silver lining, as it gave me the feeling that I was doing something for our world——our family. I have made millions since, but none of those millions gave me such happiness as my first week's earnings. I was now a helper of the family, and no longer a total charge upon my parents. Often had I heard my father's beautiful singing of 'The Boatie Rows' and often I longed to fulfil the last lines of the verse:

> When Aalick, Jock and Jeanette
> Are up and got their kair (education)
> They'll serve to gar the boatie row,
> And lichten a' our care.

To quarrel in any way with these admirable sentiments would be boorish; certainly they are not to be doubted. It is necessary to note, however, that even the quality of statement is reminiscent of the Alger hero; a tone characteristic of the whole *Autobiography* and infinitely more valuable, for the light it throws upon the author, than the sequence of facts he gives us.

After some months in the cotton-mill, Carnegie became a messenger-boy, picked up a knowledge of telegraphy, rose to the position of assistant operator and a salary of twenty-five dollars a month by the time he was seventeen. "Whenever one learns to do anything," he tells us, "he never has to wait long for an opportunity of putting his knowledge to use." In 1835, leaving the telegraph office, he went to work as operator and chief clerk for Thomas A. Scott, division superintendent of the Pennsylvania railroad; six years later, at twenty-three, he was made assistant manager at a salary of fifteen hundred dollars a year.

Thus far, as students of the Alger classics will recall, his life has paralleled almost exactly those of the heroes of *Sink or Swim, Try and Trust, Strive and Succeed*. Like them he shows the same industry, the same slow but sure rise, the same singleness of purpose. The Alger epics, however, do not carry their heroes beyond the time when, like the twenty-three-year-old Carnegie earning fifteen hundred dollars a year, their feet are firmly planted on the ladder of success. In the *Autobiography* we are privileged to follow the adventures of such a young man further——to learn what his first investment was, for example, (ten shares of Adams

Express) and what he said when he received his first dividend check: "Eureka! Here's the goose that lays the golden eggs."

We also learn, not without surprise, that after a mere six years had passed, his investments began to demand so much of his attention that he found it necessary to leave the railroad in order to look after them; investments that consisted, among others, of interests in a locomotive works, a bridge-building company, a rail-making concern, and an iron mill. Not bad, John Applegate would say; a capital young man indeed. Nor would his admiration be dimmed by the fact that all this was done on a salary which, as far as we know, never exceeded one hundred and twenty-five dollars a month; a feat of finance that might lead the innocent-minded, as Mark Sullivan has said, to look upon Carnegie as the outstanding example of Scotch thrift in all history.

Of his thrift there can be no doubt; but neither can it be doubted that the start of his fortune was like that of a number of others built up by such early railroad men as Cornelius Vanderbilt, James J. Hill, Jay Gould and James Fisk, Jr.—— fortunes fairly adequately described by the remark said to have been passed when an expensive saddle-horse was bought by a minor official: "Sired by the railroad and damned by the stockholders." It was not until the 1920's that a businessman's "contacts" were discovered to be as valuable as his intelligence or ability, perhaps more so, but such associations had their negotiability during those crowded years when the great American capitalists were hewing out their empires and staging their bronze-age battles for the economic control of a continent.

A railroad official——even a minor one, a division superintendent like Carnegie——could be a great and good friend to a rail-making company, a locomotive company, a bridge-building company, and any other company that might happen to stand along the lines. And if there was a return of favors, a sort of mutual-aid society, such was the general practice of the time. Everybody was doing it and, as in those societies where a man is automatically polygamous because all his neighbors have several wives, nobody thought it immoral. No one found fault with Carnegie for making money by taking advantage of his position with the railroad; he was probably more praised than censured. If it was not a thing Thomas Jefferson would have done, or Lincoln, or John Calhoun who turned down a badly needed loan because he suspected it was being granted for political reasons——well, as John Applegate would say, things were different. A new America was in the making, a new civilization, and the integrity of the great Americans of an earlier time——that, we might say, which lay at the heart of their greatness——was at a discount in the marts of trade.

Carnegie, with a kind of forthright naïveté, never tried to conceal the advantage he took of his position with the railroad. Writing in 1906, by which time such practices had come to be considered slightly less than ethical, he tells of meeting a man who had the novel idea of building "cars for night travel," (Pullmans), and of introducing him to his superior, Thomas A. Scott, who agreed to place two of the new cars upon the line. Whereupon the grateful inventor, Carnegie informs us, "greatly to my surprise offered me an eighth interest in the venture. I promptly accepted his offer. The first considerable sum I made was from this source."

There were other sources as well. The *Autobiography* does not go into detail on this score, but Burton J. Hendrick, in his *Life of Andrew Carnegie*, exhibits an itemized statement of income for the year 1868.

Income for 1868

Keystone Bridge Company	$15,000
Union Iron Mills	20,000
Central Transportation Company	6,000
Southern	300
Union Pacific	3,000
Furnaces	—
Rail Mill	6,000
Lochiel	400
Bitner	2,000
Columbia Oil Company	2,000
Third Bank	300
Union Line	360
Empire do (?)	450
Fort Pitt	—
Locomotive	—
North American Insurance	—
Min. & others	—
Surplus	300
	$56,110

Impressive though this record is, of greater interest is the private memorandum which accompanies it——one of the few glimpses into Carnegie's inner character that has been permitted to us.

St. Nicholas Hotel, New York.
December, 1868

Thirty-three and an income of $50,000 per annum! By this time two years I can arrange all my business as to secure at least $50,000 per annum. Beyond this never earn——make no effort to increase fortune, but spend the surplus each year for benevolent purposes. Cast aside business forever, except for others.

Settle in Oxford and get a thorough education, making the acquaintance of literary men—this will take three years' active work——pay especial attention to speaking in public. Settle then in London and purchase a controlling interest in some newspaper or live review and give the general management of it attention, taking a part in public matters, especially those connected with education and improvement of the poorer classes.

Man must have an idol——the amassing of wealth is one of the worst species of idolatry——no idol more debasing than the worship of money. Whatever I engage in I must push inordinately; therefore should I be careful to choose that life which will be the most elevating in its character. To continue much longer overwhelmed by business cares and with most of my thoughts wholly upon the way to make more money in the shortest time, must degrade me beyond hope of permanent recovery. I will resign business at thirty-five, but during the ensuing two years I wish to spend the afternoons in receiving instruction and in reading systematically.

Carnegie, on the first page of his *Autobiography*, promises to speak not as one "posturing in public," but with the utmost freedom. This promise, however, is not kept; nowhere do we find anything like the uninhibited frankness of these lines written in a hotel bedroom. And if we suspect a certain fraudulence in the *Autobiography*, a falling into that very posturing he says he wishes to avoid, our suspicions are here confirmed. The path of life was not always so clearly defined, so sunlit, as he asks us to believe. We get tired, furthermore, of having him dwell upon the high, even noble, purpose that inspired his charities. Granting his purpose was high, that it sprang from more complicated motives than a desire to buy fame, as Mark Twain thought, it is also fairly apparent that there was involved an effort to resolve an inner conflict whose roots went back to his childhood, a contrast implied between the harsh circumstances of his youth and the more palpable contingencies of material success, and that there was also present, at least to some degree, the desire to ease a troubled social conscience.

Only the irresponsible, replacing of one set of prejudices with another, would put forward this latter view as the whole explanation of Carnegie's career as a philanthropist. But this interpretation, which we associate with the debunkers, is only a normal reaction against the tone set, not only by Carnegie, but by his whole generation. To pass from the writings of the earlier Americans to those who came forward after the Civil War——from Franklin's autobiography to that of Carnegie, from the letters of Jefferson and Calhoun to those of McKinley and Mark Hanna, from the speeches of Lincoln to those of Cleveland——to make this dreary voyage is to realize, along with the appalling decline, what a premium had come to be placed on conformity and mediocrity: there are times when the Civil War seems to have been fought to make America safe for the second-rate.

It was the generation of Carnegie and Grant, obsessed with the notion that unless a reputation is spotless it cannot be heroic, that set itself to censoring the writings of the founding fathers and then went on to expurgate their characters. That Carnegie should have been influenced by this tendency is not unnatural; he, no less than the next man, wanted to appear in public with his best foot forward. This we can understand; more baffling is the fact that even his private letters, except when they deal with actual business affairs, have the same counterfeit ring. Can we really believe him, this possessor of one of the three greatest fortunes of his time, when he says "I would destroy, if I had the power, every vestige of privilege in England and give to every man equal and exact privileges"; are we to take his professed contempt of the titled classes seriously, the endless reiteration of his contumely and scorn?

"Tennyson too, bowing to such influences!" he wrote when the poet was knighted. "He stands as a miserable example——the highest art of all, poetry, is prostituted to the claims of birth. 'A weak old man,' is the verdict here. *Barren* Tennyson he has been for years. I don't want to see him now. I think Matthew Arnold would hesitate to accept such a humiliation."

Mark Twain, we suspect, would not have been fooled by such goings-on as this. It was left to Twain, in the private paper already mentioned, to paint the best portrait of Carnegie that has come down to us and to strike off the true lineaments of his character in a single brilliant phrase——The Human Being Unconcealed. "He is just like the rest of the human race but with this difference," Mark Twain wrote. "The rest of the race try to conceal what they are, and succeed, whereas Andrew tries to conceal what he is but doesn't succeed."

In a wonderful description of a visit to Carnegie's home, which in itself might stand as a partial refutation of the theory that Mark Twain was "taken in" by the respectable East, he goes on to fill in the details of his portrait.

> Mr. Carnegie is not any better acquainted with himself than if he had met himself for the first time day before yesterday. He thinks he is a rude, bluff, independent spirit, who writes his mind and thinks his mind with an almost extravagant Fourth of July independence; whereas he is really the counterpart of the rest of the human race in that he does not boldly speak his mind except when there isn't any danger in it. He thinks he is a scorner of kings and emperors and dukes, whereas he is like the rest of the human race: a slight attention from one of these can make him drunk for a week and keep his happy tongue wagging for seven years.
>
> I was there an hour or so thereabouts, and was about to go when Mr. Carnegie just happened to remember by pure accident, apparently, something which had escaped his mind——this something which had escaped his mind being, in fact, a something which had not been out of his mind for a moment in the hour and which he was perishing to tell me about.

He jumped up and said, "Oh, wait a moment. I knew there was something I wanted to say. I want to tell you about my meeting with the Emperor."

The German Kaiser, he meant. His remark brought a picture to my mind at once, a picture of Carnegie and the Kaiser; a picture of a battleship and a Brooklyn ferryboat, so to speak . . . I could see the Kaiser's bold big face, independent big face as I remember it, and I could see that other face turned up toward it——that foxy, white-whiskered, cunning little face, happy, blessed, lit up with a sacred fire, and squeaking, without words: "Am I in Heaven or is it only a dream?"

Carnegie loves to talk about his encounters with sovereigns and aristocracies; loves to talk of these splendid artificialities in a lightly scoffing and compassionate vein and try not to let on that those encounters are the most precious bric-a-brac in the treasury of his memory; but he is just a human being, and he can't even wholly deceive himself, let alone the house cat. With all his gentle scoffings, Carnegie's delight in his contacts with the great amounts to a mania; it must be as much as four years since King Edward visited him at Skibo Castle, [Carnegie's home in Scotland] yet it is an even bet that not a day has passed since then that he has not told somebody all about it. He cannot leave the King's visit alone; he has told me about it at least four times, in detail. I don't believe I can stand the King Edward visit again.

This description of the steel-master, etched in acid though it is, strikes us as having a closer resemblance to the living original than the Carnegie we meet in the pages of the *Autobiography*. There are few purported confessions that conceal so much and reveal so little: were it not for the self-communication written in the St. Nicholas Hotel, which Carnegie nowhere mentions, he would be as lifeless as a badly-joined puppet, dripping sawdust at every pore. That is the one time when we are won whole-heartedly to his side. So much are we swayed that, like a spectator carried away by the play, we wish to cry out our advice——"You're right, young man; follow your own admonitions." We would have been the material losers had he done so, for there can be but few Americans who have not in some way benefited from his purse, but, instead of libraries and grants and foundations, we might have had something more valuable——a distinct development in the American character; an inspiriting departure from the "successful" men of his generation, the group of whom Charles Francis Adams was to say so damningly, "A less interesting crowd I do not care to encounter."

For Carnegie to do this, however, given his temper and the temper of the times, was altogether impossible. His desire for wealth was greater than his desire for the good life——how can it be argued otherwise?——but it would be an error to deduce from his decision to remain in business merely a love of gain. Andrew Carnegie talked about money no less than does John Applegate——there are few books, indeed, out of the field of finance, upon whose pages the word "millions" appears more frequently than upon those of his autobiography——but to him, as to John Applegate, money was likewise a symbol and measure of success; a word, in the vocabulary of that grasping generation, that meant one thing only: power. Empires were in the making, duchies and feudal kingdoms, and while Carnegie never stopped talking of the sequestered life, he was driven by every basic impulse to the center of the arena, defending and enlarging his own domain. Early in his autobiography he tells us "nothing could be allowed to interfere with my business career for a moment," and in this almost accidental confession there is revealed the shaft and piston of his life. It has been argued, by one of his biographers, that had the iron industry not been revolutionized by the discovery that molten metal could be decarbonized by forcing a stream of air through it——the essential principle of the Bessemer process——he might have followed the road he mapped for himself in the hotel bedroom. But this is mere theorizing, a by-product of apology. The fact remains that, instead of retiring, he made use of Bessemer's discovery further to expand his industrial empire until it was the largest of its kind the world had ever seen: the iron-master became the steel-master and the face of a nation was forever changed.

As the name of John D. Rockefeller, during that era, became synonymous with oil, so did that of Carnegie become representative of steel. The one was the outstanding exponent of combination, thinking in terms of mergers and cartels, while the other, like the true troglodyte he was, hammered his way from the iron age into the steel age with the club of ruthless competition. Of the two, Rockefeller's methods were actually more humane; yet it is he, rather than Carnegie, who is remembered in American folklore as the evil genius of cruelty in business.

Rockefeller, going to other men in the oil business, would preach the desirability of combination and the wastes of competition; Carnegie, contrariwise, scorned cooperation, looking upon price-fixing agreements, for example, as "bad business . . . strengthening the other fellow as much as they strengthen you." To the governing board of the Carnegie Steel Company, he wrote: "We should look with favor upon every combination of every kind upon the part of our competitors; the bigger they grow, the more vulnerable they become." During the course of his career he acquired but two competing plants, Homestead and Duquesne; the rest of the time he harried his rivals the way the chiefs of the Scottish border raided and pillaged the lands of their English neighbors: "Carnegie's cattle-work along the border," the steel trade came to call the pitiless methods which made him, by 1900, the undisputed master of his field.

It was only then, thirty-two years after he wrote his private memorandum on the good life, when his enemies had all been routed and he himself was sixty-five and scarred with battle, that he gave serious thought to retirement.

"Our profits had reached forty millions of dollars per year and the prospect of increased earnings before us was amazing," he writes. "Steel had ascended the throne and was driving away all inferior material. It was clearly seen that there was a great future ahead; but so far as I was concerned I knew the task of distribution before me would tax me in my old age to the utmost."

To dispose of an industrial empire like the Carnegie Steel Company and its allied interests, however, required more than the mere offering of it for sale. There was, actually, but one possible purchaser——J. Pierpont Morgan, the only man in America who commanded enough wealth and financial backing to form the steel trust which must be created to purchase the Carnegie interests.

The story of the negotiations between Carnegie and the elder Morgan reads like the story of a gigantic horse-trade. Like the boy in the Lincoln fable, Carnegie set out to demonstrate that if the splints were good for his steel company, it had them; if they weren't, it didn't. And, having come by his reputation for ruthlessness honestly, he immediately built a fire under Morgan by having his press agent give out the statement that the Carnegie Company intended to erect a twelve million dollar pipe-and-tube mill that would have been in direct competition with Morgan's interests in the already existing National Tube Works. He actually bought the land on which the plant was to stand, had plans drawn up, and began work on the foundations.

Meanwhile, a steady stream of press releases came from his headquarters in Pittsburg, telling of new enterprises upon which he intended to embark. He started rumors that he was going to build a railroad in competition with the Pennsylvania, now a Morgan property, and even began surveys for a Carnegie road from Pittsburg to the Atlantic. Such rumors and announcements unsettled the whole financial world; the network of Morgan interests began to suffer; other bankers and industrial magnates begged Morgan to "do something" about Carnegie.

This application of threat and pressure, balanced by allurement in the form of glowing descriptions of the blessings of industrial peace, will be easily recognized as the "war of nerves." Carnegie's use of this strategy was described, by James Howard Bridge in his *History of the Carnegie Steel Company*, by an analogy taken from the field of religion. "In the conversion of the heathen, missionaries have found it useful to describe the condition of the damned before presenting a picture of the joys of the blessed. It was on some such principle that the threat of industrial war was thus made by Carnegie, before the blessings of cooperation and consolidation were set out before the alarmed financier."

The end of the negotiations between the elder Morgan and Carnegie's agents was reached in January, 1901, when Carnegie sold out for four hundred million; his own share, measured in cash, coming to around two hundred and fifty million. The one-time bobbin-boy, at the conclusion of the deal, received Morgan's congratulations on being the richest man in the world. This was success beyond the outermost limits of fiction: Horatio Alger himself would have rejected it as being too fantastically extreme.

The economic implications of that success, which were first suggested on March 3, 1901, when plans for organizing the United States Steel Corporation were made public by J. P. Morgan and Company, do not quite fall within the consideration of this essay. That date, however, offers itself as being hardly less important, in relation to John Applegate's America, than that which marks Columbus' discovery of the new world. The theocracy of Cotton Mather and the Pilgrim Fathers,

Thomas Jefferson's agrarian democracy, the slave-holding imperialism of John Calhoun, the fluid society of small capitalists envisioned by Abraham Lincoln——all had been swept
away. Geared to the dynamo of the industrial revolution, Big
Business had become Brobdingnagian in size. A new elect had
risen. And it was they, the financial and corporate elect, who
now insisted upon the right to rule.

"For thirty years," William Howard Taft was to say, "We
had had an enormous material expansion in this country, in
which we all forgot ourselves in the enthusiasm of expanding
our material resources and in making ourselves the richest nation on earth. We did this through the use of the principle of
organization and combination, and through the development
of our national resources. In the encouragement of the investment of capital we nearly transferred complete political power
to those who controlled corporate wealth and we were in
danger of a plutocracy."

Despite the gloomy foreboding of a large part of the press,
the conservative Boston *Herald* going so far as to conclude
that "if a limited financial group should come to represent the
capitalistic ends of industry, the perils of socialism may be
looked upon by even intelligent people as possibly the lesser
of two evils," it cannot be said that John Applegate's father,
reading of the formation of the steel trust, knew a limit had
been reached. The progressive movement was astir, and Theodore Roosevelt would soon head a rebellion against the trusts,
but John Applegate's parent was no more aware of momen-
tous change, of the flicker of heat-lightning upon the presence
of tomorrow, than was to be his son in the next generation,
sitting in his living-room listening to the radio while the tides
of an era were flowing out. He, like most Americans, had
looked upon the welter of change brought about by the machine age as a reflection of the spirit of progress. The American system, it was believed, was justifying itself by its works;

the ceaseless, dynamic onrush of the Industrial Revolution gave purposeful and tangible meaning to the idea of liberal democracy.

If John Applegate's father had any premonitions of future crisis, as did the editorial writer for the New Orleans *Picayune* who wrote, "Governments will be operated, congresses and legislatures will be continued for the express purpose of legislating for these mighty corporations, and individuals will cease to be considered. After that, what?," he could afford to shrug them aside. The future was a house other people would live in, and it was easier, much easier, to chuckle over the way Finley Peter Dunne's "Mister Dooley" summed up the drift of the times:

> Pierpont Morgan calls in wan iv his office boys, th' prisidint iv a naytional bank, an' says he, "James," he says, "take some change out iv th' damper an' r-run out an' buy Europe f'r me," he says. "I intind to re-organize it an' put it on a paying basis," he says. "Call up the Czar an' th' Pope an' th' Sultan an' th' Impror Willum, an' tell thim we won't need their sarvices afther nex' week," he says. "Give thim a year's salary in advance. An', James," he says, "Ye betther put that r-redheaded bookkeeper near th' dure in charge iv th' continent. He doesn't seem to be doin' much."

A few weeks later, on the front page of the newspaper that carried "Mister Dooley's" column, John Applegate's father read that Andrew Carnegie was going abroad. Again turning to his favorite philosopher, he found that he thought Mr. Carnegie must be a very happy man:

"He has money, he has fame, he has Andhrew Carnaygie, and he's a little deaf."

II

The notion of the "inspired millionaire," which would probably be John Applegate's way of summing up the character of Andrew Carnegie and other conspicuous examples of the success story, seems to be part of the intellectual inheritance handed down by his father, a relic of the Gilded Age. It is hard to understand, on first consideration, how this concept ever came about. Despite the fact that the merchant prince is one of the oldest human types, found in the most ancient civilizations, Emily Applegate's contrary idea that millionaires are principally valuable as exponents of Veblen's theory of "conspicuous waste," and anything but inspired, would probably find a much readier acceptance by the modern temper. Yet, as we wander through the quiet and mossy cemetery we call the Gilded Age, we come upon monument after monument raised to those men Emily Applegate looks upon as conscienceless plunderers who left only a track of waste and ruin. The monuments are neglected now——a fallen slab here, a chipped angel there, the wire skeletons of floral decorations rusting in the weeds——but the testaments of admiration engraved by an earlier time are still clearly to be read. Here is one extolled as an empire-builder; here another is commemorated as the benefactor of his country; here is a column carved with the words of Walt Whitman: "Business shall be, nay is, the word of the modern hero."

The conflict that exists between Emily's point of view and that of her father is more than part of the larger conflict that is almost inevitable between two different generations. It stems, in its essentials, from the mutually antagonistic terms of John Applegate's notion itself——a confusion, however, not to be laid to uncritical muddle-headedness alone. For even if we agree with Emily and Matthew Josephson that the robber-barons were sometimes hard to distinguish from a pack of dinosaurs——drinking up oil, gorging on iron and coal, destroying great forests with lashes of their tails——we are still faced with the undeniable fact that they were the most interesting phenomena of their era. The tracks they left in time have not yet been sufficiently rid of unpleasant associations to make them desirable as hearthstones, as are those actual dinosaur tracks sold in a corner of western Massachusetts, but as we take their measurements in the hope of understanding the structure and habits of the creatures who made them, we come to appreciate that the interest they aroused, even the fascination, lies not in what they were, for here the verdict of Charles Francis Adams still stands, but in what they did. It is still impossible, for example, to look upon that part of the native landscape ploughed up during the titanic struggle waged by Harriman and Schiff against Morgan and Hill for control of the Northern Pacific railroad without being struck by awe; here, we realize, was a battle of giants.

Looking at this struggle through John Applegate's eyes—— or, better, through the eyes of his father——we come to perceive, particularly if we remember that the American philosophy of moral materialism has tended increasingly to become more material than moral, that the notion of the "inspired millionaire" is not without a certain validity. These were the men ——the Vanderbilts, the Harrimans, the Carnegies, the Jim Fisks——who gave drama and excitement to the times. As the political struggles of the years before the Civil War were followed with the interest that now attaches itself to a pennant-race, so were the struggles of the great capitalists during the Gilded Age. The battle for possession of the Northern Pacific, which in one day forced the price of its shares from one hundred ninety to over one thousand dollars, was watched with as much excitement as a World Series. John Applegate, consequently, in talking about an "inspired millionaire," is using the word in the same context as when he talks about an "inspired" ballplayer——Babe Ruth, for instance, was clearly visited by inspiration the day he hit three home-runs.

A moralist, however, confirmed in his tendencies, would

feel called upon to quarrel with John Applegate for being unaware that his ideal of an "inspired millionaire" implies a disinterested man, an obviously contradictory notion. He would have to point out, as Van Wyck Brooks has done, that any social ideal must stand or fall on whether or not it provides a possible moral program for the individual; a way of looking at life, a point of view—which, of course, the ideal of millionairedom does not; consisting, as it does, merely of the determination to get hold of a million dollars. Going further, the moralist might find in these idealisms of John Applegate, the "inspired millionaire" and the "inspired ball-player," a certain spiritual paucity, a lack of standards and values, a bleak indifference to the non-material world.

But John Applegate, who is simply a citizen of a particular culture, is here as much in need of understanding as criticism. If he finds his set of standards and values in the realm of business, and regards the millionaire as a more than serviceable social ideal, it is because business, from the end of the Civil War to the present time, has been the most absorbing activity of American life. Even Van Wyck Brooks, one of the severest critics of our business civilization, is forced to this admission.

"The idealization of business in America," he writes in *Three Essays on America*, "has a certain validity which elsewhere it could not have. One cannot compare the American commercial type with the commercial type that England has evolved without feeling in the latter a certain fatty degeneration, a solemn, sanctified, legalized self-satisfaction, which our agile, free, open, though sometimes indefinitely more unholy type is quite without; for even in his unholiness the unholy business man in America is engagingly crooked rather than ponderously corrupt . . . a gay, sprightly, childlike being, moved and movable, the player of a game, a sportsman essentially, though with a frequently dim perception of the rules. . . . Business has traditionally ab-

sorbed the best elements of the American character . . .
Just those elements which in other countries produce
art and literature, formulate the ideals and methods of
philosophy and sociology, think and act for those disinterested ends which make up the meaning of life; just
that free, disinterested, athletic sense of play which is
precisely the same in dialectic, in art, in religion, in
sociology, in sport——just these, relatively speaking, have
in America been absorbed in trade. It is not remarkable
that, on the one hand, our thought and literature are so
perfunctory while, on the other, American business is
so seductive, so charming, so gay an adventure."

Even though we may feel that Brooks has here surveyed
the field of American business from the same lofty plane he
sometimes accuses Emerson of having dwelled upon, and
like Walt Whitman is unable altogether to make up his mind
whether he admires or deplores the commercial emphasis of
American life, the impression is that he is perhaps more
nearly correct in this passage of diagnosis than in those given
over solely to anger and excoriation. For the fact is that
when literary men find fault with the material aspect of our
culture, and criticize it, they are merely decrying something
inherently alien to the literary point of view——a point of
view, more precisely, which has somehow drifted outside the
main channel and current of American life.

This conflict of standards and values, roughly indicated
by John Applegate's division of all human brows into the two
fixed classes of high and low, has been latent in the American
complex ever since the first transplanted Europeans began to
push back the geographical frontier from the Atlantic to the
Pacific. "Never have metaphysics or Aristotelian logic," said
one learned colonist, "earned a loaf of bread." When John
Applegate's great-uncle was busy killing Indians, clearing
the forest, and raising his house with his own hands, a good
axe and a good rifle were of far more value to him than all

the culture of the ages. The pioneer not only had no time or opportunity to acquire manners and culture, but, as James Truslow Adams remarks in his study *Our Business Civilization*, because of the apparent uselessness of manners and culture, he came to despise them. They marked the soft and effeminate, the dandy, whereas he and his companions were the "real men," the fellows who really counted. "The well-dressed, cultured person," writes Adams, "becomes the 'dude,' an object of derision, who, so far from exerting any ameliorating social or intellectual influence, is heartily looked down upon; and culture itself is relegated to idle women as something with which no real man would concern himself."

This passage has the same look of alarm that crosses the faces of most scholars when they contemplate the American scene——a panorama that has been variously described as jungle, wasteland, and agitated by the jitters——but in its broad outlines the geodesy is correct. What is most impressive about such evaluations of our American culture, however, is that they in themselves stand as evidence of the unhappy division of which their authors complain——a bill of divorcement granted more on grounds of mutual incompatibility than actual neglect or cruelty.

Such incompatibility has always been present. If John Applegate tends to look upon the poet and the painter as intellectual dudes, wearing loosely-draped clothes that indicate loosely-draped morals, they, for their part, look upon him much as Emerson looked upon the young Southerner he wrote about in his *Journal*——"In civil, educated company, where anything human is going forward, he is dumb and unhappy, like an Indian in a church."

Yet despite this long record of mutual suspicion, the earlier American writers, those who participated in the great literary period of New England, were able to feel themselves fairly central to their place and time: as men of culture they too had a role to play. It is only when we reached the Gilded Age, the era of the "inspired millionaire," that we find the conflict between the artist and society so deepening as to create the almost unbridgeable gap that exists today. The hordes of young people who fled America in the 1920's, and went to Europe in search of a climate more favorable to the green shoots of the artistic impulse, apparently thought themselves, as would appear from Malcolm Cowley's memoir, *The Exile's Return*, rebels and pathfinders. They were, in fact, merely following a trail first broken by James Whistler and Henry James.

The early American writers had always looked abroad—— to England, to the Mediterranean countries, to the near and far East. Never, however, did they renounce America as their spiritual homeland. Whatever was taken from abroad——seen, read, tasted, heard——was introduced into the native fabric and given native emphasis and interpretation. The New Englander of the first half of the Nineteenth Century was inspired, as Edmund Wilson has said in *The Triple Thinkers*, "to present the world with a new humanity, set free from the caste-barriers and poverties of Europe, which should return to the mother country only to plunder her for elements of culture which might contribute to the movement at home." Later, with the triumph of industrialism, and the ascendency of the millionaire to the central place in the American solar system, the persons who were concerned with thought and culture began to disavow the United States and take refuge in Europe.

This withdrawal on the part of the artist from American life——a negative instead of a positive reaction: a rejection of Emerson's credo, "Nerve us with incessant affirmatives"—— was to have disastrous consequences. John Applegate, at a time when he stood most in need of the scholar and the poet, the man of culture, would be left open and unprotected against the intellectual barbarities of a later era. And the man of culture, having rejected John Applegate as unworthy, able for the most part to perform no better act of husbandry than to scatter an already thin and acid soil with the compost of contempt, the artist, in his turn, was to float about like a petticoat-creeper on the wind——part of two worlds but belonging to neither.

Nowhere is this divorce of the artist from society given a more decided emphasis than in the life of Henry James. James' act of expatriation was, in its essence, a revolt against the success story; though to talk of him as having uprooted himself from America, as is generally done, is not altogether correct. James had traveled so much in his earlier years that he had no firmly established sense of place: he was no more a child of Boston than he was of London or New York. What we find in his novels is not so much a dispute between two sets of values, European and American, as a reflection of the harsh and puzzling contradictions of the Gilded Age. As Wilson points out, James shows us all that was magnanimous, invigorating and human in the American character, along with all that was frustrated, sterile and emotionally meager——the sort of spiritual starvation that Carnegie unwittingly reveals in the letter written to himself in the bedroom of the St. Nicholas hotel.

What James is doing, in his role as social historian, is to show us the effect of the success story upon the men and women of his era. What has happened to make them so wan? "Well," Wilson concludes, speaking for James, "they have become very rich, and being rich is a terrible burden; in the process of getting rich they have starved themselves spiritually at home; and now that they are trying to get something for their money, they find that they have put themselves at the mercy of all the schemers and adventurers of Europe."

Carnegie's autobiography, left unfinished at his death,

ends with an episode that gives vivid confirmation to this side of James' point of view. Telling of the presentation in 1912 of a testimonial to the German Emperor in celebration of twenty-five years of peace, Carnegie wonders if the Kaiser "will rise to his appointed mission as The Apostle of Peace," and tells Wilhelm, in that fustian fashion of his, "In this noblest of all missions you are our chief ally." What character, in James, is quite so gullible as this? The "inspired millionaire" turns out to be more simple than the heroine of *Daisy Miller*, without having her fresh and wayward American charm. Even she, we feel, who knew no better than to compromise her reputation, would have managed to meet the outbreak of the War of 1914-18 with a deeper sense of reality than Carnegie who, to conclude his life-story, can only cry out: "Watch President Wilson! He has Scotch blood in his veins!"

What makes Henry James valuable as a guide to the era of the great millionaires is that his own career, like that of Mark Twain, had been greatly affected by the change in the national culture that took place after the Civil War. Just as the aspirations of the democratic frontier were affronted in Mark Twain, stinging him to the satire of *The Gilded Age* and *A Connecticut Yankee In King's Arthur's Court*, so were the aspirations of New England's golden age affronted in James by the cruder aspirations of the success story——a general philosophy which, with an irony some may find amusing, had its roots in the same soil that produced the Concord renaissance.

The Puritan emphasis upon the virtues of industry and thrift had always been underscored, and, in addition, there was always the implied bond between supernatural approval and worldly success. The sage of Concord himself, whose saintly transcendentalism swathed a hard core of Yankee shrewdness, found that "Success has no more eccen-

tricity than the gingham and muslin we weave in our mills";
and Timothy Dwight, from his eminence as president of
Yale University, brought the argument one step further and
declared "the love of property to a certain degree seems indispensable to the existence of sound morals"—the whole of
which Lowell summed up by saying: "Protestantism had made
its fortune and no longer protested."

III

While the bracketing of the novels of Horatio Alger with
those of Henry James as "representative" of the late Nineteenth Century may seem representative only of absurdity,
nonetheless, in Alger's one hundred and nineteen titles, we
have the obverse side of the era's coin.

On the popular juvenile level, before the Alger success
story come along to dispute their popularity, the dime novel
was staple fare. The standard hero of the dime novel, as John
Applegate will always remember, was Buffalo Bill; long-
haired, wearing a mustache and small goatee, "the finest
figure of a man that ever sat a steed." Thundering from adventure to adventure in more than one thousand ten-cent
melodramas, this buckskin Superman always managed to
keep his horse one nose ahead of the lathered pony ridden
by the cowboy "bad man" who rivaled him in popular favor—a gun-toting desperado who robbed banks and stage-
coaches, shot it out with posses, and made it a habit to die
with his boots on.

An understanding of the value of thrift and industry, plus
a set of copybook maxims, would seem poor weapons with
which to challenge the leadership of such energetic men of
action. This, however, is precisely what the Alger hero managed to do, attaining a popularity never matched before or
since. Perhaps the bad man and Buffalo Bill would have been
worsted in any case, but it seems more likely that the tre-

mendous vogue of the Alger series would not have been possible had it not been for the implied moral excellence of the acquisitive instinct then running wild as an unbroken pinto. One of Alger's earliest titles, *Work and Win*, reducing the accepted formula for material achievement to its lowest possible terms, was the general burden of them all——a ceaseless flow of sermons that saw the path of righteousness as the way to wealth and the love of money at the root of all good. Horatio Alger, the high priest of the success cult, was simply Timothy Dwight acting and speaking on a lower level.

The son of a domineering Unitarian minister, Alger was a neurotic youth with an obsession about sex purity who was nicknamed "Holy Horatio" by his schoolmates. After going to Harvard, where as a freshman he changed lodgings after he came across his landlady in a loose negligeé, he visited Paris and, as the cynical will have already suspected, managed to get himself seduced almost immediately by a night-club singer who taught him to sing and to dance for *lagniappe*. Out of this fertile experience, baffling as it may seem to John Applegate, came his hunger and reverence for success.

"I want to live to be great," he confessed to his diary. "Suppose it is vain——all great men are vain. What have they got that I need, to be like them? Whatever it is I will see."

Herbert Mayes, in his biography of Alger, suggests that he wrote for boys because he could not write for men——an implication of arrested development that is more than confirmed by the facts of his life. Forswearing tobacco and alcohol with the same fervor displayed by his heroes, his only habitual vice was eating candy; he also liked to play with building-blocks, follow the engines that clanged to the fires which then regularly illuminated the New York scene, and play the drum in newsboys' parades. Yet this was the man who, in his serial *Ragged Dick*, wrote what was perhaps the first American success story, as we now understand it, and created, in the person of his hero, a shabby but sterling newsboy, the stock figure of the "inspired millionaire" legend.

That Horatio Alger was an arrested adolescent is important to no one. But was there, is there, the same implication of adolescence, the same lack of human and moral education, in the cult he served so faithfully—in John Applegate's concept of the "inspired millionaire" he did so much to create? There would seem to be no other conclusion. We are told of these vessels of inspiration, even as we are told of Andrew Carnegie, that they remained "young men" to the end of their days. It is precisely this youngness, however, this lack of moral and intellectual development, that finally reveals their true character and invalidates their usefulness as an adequate social ideal. After the obvious indictment has been drawn, and outrage satisfied, the larger, more appalling judgment remains. In some form or other the dinosaurian capitalists of the Gilded Age were all Alger heroes, fixed by the beady hypnotic eye of material success, and it was the tragedy of such a hero, as it was of his creator, never to grow up. If their monuments were to go down to ruin, and later generations find it impossible to do them homage, it would be only because the nation, howsoever slowly it crawled along the road to maturity, seeking a more salient individual and social interest and a more vital method of life, would come in time to need a larger inspiration than they could hope to provide.

·6·

P. T. BARNUM SITS FOR A PORTRAIT
The American As Educator

LOOK FROM the mold-shattering face of Abraham Lincoln, its very perfection of homeliness giving it that quality of authority Henry James once described as "commanding style"——turn from this mask of American uniqueness to a photograph of Phineas Taylor Barnum and you discover the face of the American average.

John Applegate, pledged to his set of stock responses, would immediately recognize it as such. A "typical" face he would call it, comfortable to have around, a face whose shape and character bears the unmistakable impress of the large American die. The broad fleshy nose, the wide full mouth with its suggestion of a coin-purse, the eyes set deep beneath a jut of bushy brow, the high domed forehead crested by a fringe of curly hair——all stamp him as a member of the "ingroup," the multitudinous unremarkable norm. The cartoonist's pencil might be tempted, as it frequently was during his lifetime, but not the artist's brush. Only the ears, for one brief moment, might hold the artist's attention——great protruding flaps of ears, exaggerated as Cyrano's beak, ears that would indicate their possessor (if the folk-way interpretation of big ears is correct) as one of the most generous and expansive of men.

And so he was. Hanging above a mantel in the house of one of his descendants is a photograph that shows him surrounded by the members of his family; daughters, sons-in-law, grandchildren, great-grandchildren. The large humanity of the beaming patriarch still warms the fading print; even the swell of his paunch gives off an aura of geniality and good-will——we would know him, without any further evidence, as an eminently social creature.

To be a social creature is perhaps implied in the circus-man's career. Barnum, however, liked people to stream through the doors of his home as much as he enjoyed having them pass through the gates of his American Museum. He knew every-body, prince and pauper, bishop and Bowery bum, and for company's sake the one was as good as the other. "As a host he could not be surpassed," Gamaliel Bradford quotes one of his visitors as saying. "He knew the sources of comfort—— what to omit doing, as well as what to do, for a guest. He had the supreme art of making you feel really free, as if you were in your own home."

Whatever plumb-lines Barnum dropped into the depths of the human character did not go very deep: he knew, however, perhaps was born with the knowledge, that in laughter and credulity all men are alike. William and Henry James were frequent visitors to the American Museum on Saturday after-noons during their boyhood, and Henry Ward Beecher, lately arrived in Brooklyn, wandered through the maze of curiosities that were on display. And as the crowds swarmed through the chambers, Barnum would leave the platform to jest and fraternize with his patrons just as he fraternized and jested with Mark Twain and Matthew Arnold and the Bishop of London. Everything we know about him, in the social sphere, lends confirmation to the various appreciations of his human worth that have come down to us——particularly the gentle tribute written by his second wife as a supplement to the last edition of his autobiography: a book first published in 1855 as *The Life of P. T. Barnum, Written by Himself,* and subsequently reprinted, with added new chapters, almost as regularly as *The Farmer's Almanac.*

The portraitist, looking closer, might find in the face of this average American traces of a certain vanity——an aggressive thrust toward reputation betrayed by a vigorous thrust of jaw. Why, otherwise, this constant flow of autobiographies, year after year? "Without printer's ink," Barnum confesses in his *Life,* "I would have been no bigger than Tom Thumb." With printer's ink, by shouting the wonders of his attractions from the early days when he was exhibiting Joice Heth (*"The Greatest Natural & National Curiosity In The World . . . AGE OF 161 YEARS . . . Nurse to Gen. George Washington, the Father of our Country"*)——from these struggling charlatan days to the high period of Tom Thumb and Jenny Lind, he used printer's ink to draw millions to his ticket-window and a fortune to himself. Did he hope, then, by this same token, and with a sort of vulgar egotism, to set out his autobiographies like pots of honey, drawing posterity's bees? Or did this steady stream have its origin in the headwaters of his every inspiration: the bare and brassy credo which held all advertising to be good advertising, even when one was publicly called a humbug.

"It's a great thing to be called a humbug," he proclaimed. "It means hitting the public in reality. Anybody who can do so, is sure to be called a humbug by somebody who can't."

Egotism there was, large and undeniable, and if it seems more brazen than that of a hundred other men whose self-preoccupation likewise flowered into autobiography, it is largely because we prefer our egotism as the mid-Victorians preferred the legs of their women——decently covered, draped twenty inches below the knee. Nor did Barnum ever make use of the basic autobiographical fiction: that, instead of being a form of catharsis, not altogether unlike the Catholic ritual of confession, it is a lesson in the way of life. There are maxims enough in his autobiography, and conscientious liftings of the pointer toward "the higher things," but at no time is this permitted to interfere with the actual business at hand. The title he finally settled upon for the later editions of his life-story was *Struggles and Triumphs;* in the interests of accuracy, however, he might better have used a heading from one of its chapters—"The Art of Money Getting." This was the craft he practiced all his life, as an energetic Connecticut Yankee should, and for all the egotism implied by his long line of autobiographies, they are more correctly taken as evidences of his extreme devotion to the only art he knew. The art of life was something he never stopped to dwell upon, having in his bustling fashion no time to stop and meditate upon the ideal aspects of material things, and, if he had, he would have seen it as part and parcel of the other, more urgent art—that of getting money in the bank.

Yet, as in the case of John Applegate, this frank affection for gain was not inspired by a love of money alone. Barnum talked about money as much as anyone, his last question on man's mortal earth being "What were the receipts yesterday?" but in this he was being merely the American average, finding in the clink of coin on coin the sound that success makes. The American has always disliked the miser, even in New England where the power of the penny has never been questioned or misunderstood, and in Barnum's scale of moral values hoarding was an evil. The opulence of "Iranistan," the Oriental palace he built near Bridgeport, where elk and reindeer pranced through the park while a more astonishing elephant was hitched to a plough and sent to the fields where it could be seen from the passing railroad cars and thus advertise its owner's circus——this shrewd and elegant splendor was but an out-size indication of a liking for lavishness he had from the start. If he wanted money, and he did, it was largely because somewhere in the sound that success makes there was the sound of fame——the larger hope, the more compelling dream, was for a name and reputation that might be blown, as through the trumpet of Chatterton's angel, clear across the world.

This hope, in his own lifetime, he came to realize. The European mind of that period, crowded with the legend of the American millionaire, also found room for the legend of "Mister" Barnum. The steel master of Skibo Castle might have the King of England to visit, and be a guest on the Kaiser's yacht, but only Barnum could provoke a national crisis in English life by purchasing the elephant Jumbo from the Royal Zoological Garden. The London *Times* thundered, Jumbo became a subject of parliamentary debate, the editor of the London *Daily Telegraph* cabled: "All British children distressed at elephant's departure. Hundreds of correspondents beg us to inquire on what terms you will kindly return Jumbo." Fame could bring him to no higher pinnacle than this, from whose eminence he cabled in reply, "My compliments to Editor *Daily Telegraph* and British Nation. Fifty-one millions of American citizens anxiously awaiting Jumbo's arrival. My forty years' invariable practice of exhibiting the best that money could procure, makes Jumbo's presence here imperative. My largest tent seats thirty thousand persons, and is filled twice each day. Wishing long life and prosperity to British Nation and *Telegraph* and Jumbo." —and if, in this straining of a ringmaster's lungs, we detect the peculiarly American confusion of notoriety with fame, we are merely observing one of the lesser results of his influence as an educator.

As the founder of the institution of the modern American circus, Barnum's claim to our present attention is slight; the important part he played in widening the scope of the American theatre is likewise of limited interest. His early adventures and disappointments, the lean years of Joice Heth and Colonel Fremont's "Wooly Horse," the time he advertised a "free buffalo hunt" on the shores of Hoboken and made a one-day killing by chartering the only ferryboats that could accommodate the amusement-hungry crowds, the way he emptied the American Museum of its slow-moving patrons one particularly busy afternoon by hanging up a sign that read "This Way To The EGRESS," his triumphal tours with Tom Thumb and Jenny Lind——these would have only an antiquarian value did they not represent stages in the progress of an education which was profoundly to affect the education of John Applegate.

The story of Barnum's life, told by himself in his autobiography and in M. R. Werner's full-length portrait, is as decided a success story as that of Andrew Carnegie——the rise from rags to riches is no less marked. It is impossible, however, to fit Barnum into the standard Alger hero mold. To have acquired the title of "Prince of Humbugs" was damaging enough——to have basked in the reputation, and made use of it as part of his stock in trade, put him forever beyond the pale. Yet Barnum's career, when ranged next to that of the great plunderers who gave the era its moral tone, is almost shining in its honesty. There is no question that he made use of some palpable fakes in the early part of his career, as he himself confesses, but during a lifetime spent in the show-business his out-and-out hoaxes do not number a dozen. The fact is that the dubious reputation which clings to his name in the American mythology, summed up in the dictum "There's one born every minute," is actually a distorted shadow of his peculiar mercantile genius. It is apt to be forgotten that, until the advent of Barnum, trickery and fraud were accepted features of the show business——the coming of the circus, particularly in the provinces, being practically synonymous with the coming of a riot. Barnum, operating against this background and heritage of distrust, carried his hoaxes just far enough to combine the maximum amount of publicity with the minimum amount of unfavorable criticism. "Advertising sky-rockets," he called them—— and there, in that one phrase, he sums up his great contribution as an American educator and gives us the principal lesson of his own.

"Such a school would 'cut eye teeth,'" he said of the academy he attended, the one that John Applegate would call the school of hard knocks, "but if it did not cut conscience, morals and integrity up by the roots, it would be because the scholars quit before their education was completed."

By this definition, Barnum was not so proficient a scholar as the Carnegies, the Vanderbilts, the Jim Fisks——they were the prize pupils, he the average. It is precisely this averageness, however, that enables him to sum up the true character of the Gilded Age, gold on top and brass beneath, and also to reveal the workings of its ordinary mind. Barnum was a millionaire, and, by John Applegate's careless rule of thumb, he too was "inspired"——his *Struggles And Triumphs* is the story of one "inspiration" after the other. But, unlike most of the records left by the successful men of his time, nearly all of which take the form of self-apology, it is singularly free of that unbecoming posturing which suggests they had all taken Horatio Alger at face value and were trying to conform to the measurements of his standard hero. Whether out of an honesty that was undoubtedly his, or whether out of pride in his genius as a showman, Barnum made no such pretenses. That he wanted to be remembered by posterity is clear enough: it is no less clear that, if he was so going to be remembered, he wished to be recalled, not as the hero of *From Rags To Riches*, but as "The Prince Of Humbugs" ——a title he invented and was the first to apply to himself.

It is true, as one of Barnum's biographers has said, that in starting the humbug legend he lighted a blaze that later he wished he could quench. Yet, as we read his autobiography, detecting the relish with which the stories of humbugging are told, it becomes fairly apparent that he found his title embarassing only on those few occasions he stepped out of his showman's role——when, for example, he was persuaded to run for Congress and was defeated, possibly by fraud, more probably because a majority of the electorate agreed with *The New York Nation* that he would be more at home in The American Museum than in the legislative halls of Washington.

As a businessman, however, Barnum never lost sight of the cash value of his title——perhaps the first American advertising slogan ever invented. It is as a businessman that P. T. Barnum has a special importance for John Applegate and, as a businessman, John Applegate will admire him for his advertising shrewdness——"The Prince of Humbugs" takes rank with *Ask The Man Who Owns One* and *The Pause That Refreshes*. Also, in the warmth of this same appreciation, John Applegate will find the ripest fruit of Barnum's education, his lecture and essay on *The Art of Money Getting*, an infinitely more compelling document, in relation to this world's work, than almost any other that has come from an American pen.

The art of money getting, despite a general opinion to the contrary, is no more an American esthetic than the art of getting into bed; man's acquisitive instinct is not an ingredient of nationalism. Nor, in our domestic history, has the art of money getting ever been anything less than the major activity of American life——the *Mayflower* and the *Susan Constant*, no less than the covered wagon, carried as part of their cargoes a substantial hope of material gain.

As other pastures are invariably greener to the eye, so are

other materialisms. Our love for Paris is likely to obscure the fact that the French imagination rarely ignores the value of the *sou*, and a delight in the English countryside makes us forgetful that the pulse-beat of Empire is but the pulse of trade. Likewise, if we find in earlier periods of our history a less commercial way of life——the Golden Age of Boston when blacksmiths wrote Latin and dairymaids quoted Greek; the ante-bellum South where conversation was an art, and leisure a natural right of the correctly placed and pigmented man——there is at work something of the same psychology, not altogether the psychology of myth, that makes dead heroes the best heroes and lost times happier than the moment's troubled and disjointed maze.

All we can say of the Gilded Age, therefore, during which time the pattern of John Applegate's business civilization began visibly to be fixed, is that there came to be applied a different stress, the emphasis of the success story, and that business, instead of being looked upon as perhaps the most desirable career for the enterprising American, was now regarded as the only career a proper American could possibly consider for himself. And the businessman, finding himself in the center of the stage, seeking greatness and having greatness thrust upon him, soon became the dominant power in the life of the nation and almost alone in his exercise of social, economic and political controls.

This shift in emphasis was protested by the more cultured and sensitive Americans of the time——notably Henry James and Mark Twain, even though the latter tried to make his peace with it, with Henry Adams wrapping his dislike of the new capitalistic civilization about himself like a cloak and seeking refuge in the Twelfth Century——but the general standards and values of the new plutocratic society, despite a background of insurgency implied by the political challenge of the Populists, became the accepted standards and values of society at large. It fell to P. T. Barnum, showman and humbug, to give those standards and values their best and most straightforward articulation. John Applegate thinks of him only in terms of the circus, attended by great beasts and diminutive people, riding in a dazzling chariot drawn by six white horses with plumes and gilded hooves. But in *The Art Of Money Getting* Barnum gave expression to a shrewd and canny credo that is still recognizable, in its larger outlines, as the general philosophy of American business.

An enterprising publisher, one of those who help nourish the native passion for self-improvement, might do well to rescue this document from the sink of antiquarianism into which it has fallen. Written as early as 1859, it still speaks in John Applegate's natural language, of a subject close to his heart——how to influence customers and win profits. Like a surveyor pushing into uncharted territory, Barnum proceeded to draw a detailed map of the fabulous country of success and lay down a set of rules for the guidance of those who hoped to exploit it, much as did Captain John Smith in his *Advice For The Inexperienced Planter*. The Puritan philosophy of material achievement, born of piety and the immediate urgencies of frontier life, passing through Benjamin Franklin and Ralph Waldo Emerson, handed down by Timothy Dwight and others to Horatio Alger, given its most spectacular expression in the careers of the dinosaurian capitalists, becomes, in Barnum, the stripped and practical commercial creed that lies at the base of John Applegate's business civilization. *The Art Of Money Getting*, it might be said, stands in much the same relation to modern industrial-commercial America as the Declaration of Independence to the revolutionary period, and John Calhoun's *Disquisition On Government* to the slave imperialism of the Old South.

Beginning with the importance of economy, the incalculable

value of a balanced budget, Barnum next stresses the value of good health. "The foundation of success in life is good health," he explains, speaking in a tone identical with that of those magazine publishers whose belief in the power of the human muscle is as a belief in the power of God. "A person cannot accumulate a fortune very well when he is sick. He has no ambition; no incentive; no force. Of course, there are those who have bad health and cannot help it; you cannot expect that such persons can accumulate wealth; but there are a great many in poor health who need not be so."

Then, after mentioning the injurious effects of tobacco and alcohol, both of which he abhorred, he proceeds to lay down a blueprint of success and explain its every detail.

"Don't Mistake Your Vocation," he warns, anticipating all those who were to make a career of vocational guidance; "Select The Right Location," he advises, more than a half-century ahead of those commercial scientists who discovered that pedestrians might be counted in order to determine the "locational" value of one street-corner above another; "Don't Get Above Your Business," he urges, dwelling on the dangers of over-expansion; "Be Systematic," he says, laying down the whole set of rules now promulgated by manufacturers of office records and business machines; "Be Polite And Kind To Your Customers," he advises, speaking like an instructor at a training-school for shop-girls. *The Art Of Money Getting*, in brief, recites nearly the whole litany of modern business folklore and practice. Whole textbooks have been written in elaboration of Barnum's maxims, and colleges of commerce and business administration founded in order to give his rough doctrine a more academic statement, but the skeletal structure is there. Barnum the circus-master is a colorful figure in American folklore; Barnum the businessman is vibrantly and significantly alive.

It is only when we reach his dissertation on advertising,

however, which occupies a substantial portion of his esthetic discourse, that we come to a full realization of his influence upon John Applegate and the mores of American business civilization. If the great capitalists of the Nineteenth Century established the economic pattern of contemporary society, central to which has been a ceaseless competition for profit and prestige, Barnum, practically unaided, created its cultural atmosphere. That he is the father of modern advertising needs no further insistence——merely to place a creation of his matured advertising instinct next to one of the ordinary "public notices" of his day is enough to comprehend that, out of a wedding of the circus and the New England commercial instinct, was born a new and generic art which, forever after, was to be the most beguiling maidservant of business, teaching a nation to want things it did not need and throw away other things it could still use.

And as the forces set loose by the Civil War gained in ever-increasing momentum, with managerial sovereignty being transferred from the owner-operator to the businessman director of capital control, as the riches of a domain were fed to the machine with one real thought only, the thought of profit, and turned into a stupendous array of goods that an ambitious and energetic people eagerly seized upon along their march to the highest standard of material living the world had ever seen, the trumpets of P. T. Barnum became the trumpets of the modern age. Every lesson learned in his school was brought to bear upon a new experiment in education, the sole purpose of which, however cunningly its hidden motive was concealed, was to teach John Applegate to want——to want, and want, and want again; a celebration of appetite never more nobly expressed than by an American president who, at the flood-stage of a material prosperity such as the world is not likely soon to see again, looked into the mists of the

American dream and found, at the end of the pursuit of happiness, two automobiles in every garage and a chicken in every pot.

Of education there are as many definitions as there are educators; the groves of académie are noisy with debate. And whether or not education has failed, in Jefferson's political sense that only through education can the people discharge their responsibility as guardians of their own freedom, (the heart of the democratic idea), or in the larger, more philosophical sense of those who, like Thomas Huxley and John Henry Newman, see education as that which gives a man a clear, conscious view of his own opinions and judgments, teaching him to see things as they are, to detect what is sophistical and discard what is irrelevant——to think, in short; to be a rounded human being——this deeper and noisier quarrel escapes the halls of the universities and is debated in the public forum of the newspapers and magazines.

Yet regardless of the failure or success of the American educational system, from kindergarten to doctor's oral, it is impossible to escape the fact that, whatever benefit John Applegate has derived from it, his principal instruction has largely been gained from those who carry Barnum's torch—— the advertisers, the publicity people, the geniuses of promotion. This reality shouts itself from the marquee of every motion-picture theatre, from the pages of every newspaper, from every political platform the length and breadth of the land. Do churches install radios? Do colleges find it financially profitable to develop championship football teams? Do authors autograph their books in department stores? Is the name of a president of the United States cried out at a political convention in a voice from the sewers? Each emphatic affirmative is a tribute to Barnum's eminence as an educator, a recognition of the widespread influence of his major contribution to John Applegate's American culture.

Having discovered the principle of showmanship, it is only proper that Barnum himself be permitted to explain how it works.

"Genin, the hatter," he recalls in his autobiography," bought the first Jenny Lind ticket at auction for two hundred and twenty-five dollars because he knew it would be a good advertisement for him. 'Who is the bidder?' said the auctioneer, as he knocked down the ticket at Castle Garden. 'Genin, the hatter,' was the response. Here were thousands of people from Fifth Avenue, and from distant cities in the highest stations of life. 'Who is Genin, the hatter?' they exclaimed. They had never heard of him before. The next morning the newspapers and telegraph had circulated the facts from Maine to Texas, and from five to ten million people had read that the tickets sold at auction for Jenny Lind's first concert amounted to about twenty thousand dollars, and that a single ticket was sold at two hundred and twenty-five dollars to 'Genin, the hatter.'

"Men throughout the country involuntarily took off their hats to see if they had a 'Genin' hat on their heads. At a town in Iowa it was found that in the crowd around the Post Office, there was one man who had a 'Genin' hat, and he showed it in triumph, although it was worn out and not worth two cents. Another man in the crowd, who seemed to envy the good fortune of the man who owned the hat, said 'Come, give us all a chance. Put it up at auction!' He did so, and it was sold as a keepsake for nine dollars and fifty cents. What was the consequence to Mr. Genin? He sold ten thousand extra hats per annum, the first six years!"

It was the Genins of the world who had Barnum's chief respect, the men who bought two hundred and twenty-five dollar tickets at public auctions and put up signs saying DON'T READ THE OTHER SIDE, (what an inspiration that was!, he thought) and he borrowed from them freely and frankly, polishing and refining their methods until he had fashioned the "science" of advertising that John Applegate tends to look upon as the modern alchemy that turns all things into gold.

Barnum himself regarded it as having certain cabalistic properties; whenever he speaks of advertising, which he regarded merely as a junior partner of showmanship, his voice takes on a quality almost of superstitious awe. It is to be noticed, particularly, that his sole aim in advertising, his fixed and constant goal, was to get himself talked about. There was no rarity so rare but that his name managed to precede it—it was not Jumbo, but "Mister Barnum's Jumbo"; not Jenny Lind, but "Mister Barnum Presents The Swedish Nightingale." It would seem that he instinctively understood the basic principle of advertising, equally the basic principle of propaganda—keep it simple, key it to the lowest level of the human understanding, repeat it again and again.

The advertising instinct was so central to Barnum's personality, so close to the heart of everything he did or said, that there are times when he gives the impression of having no private character—we are constantly reminded of one of those film people who are always trying to live up to the specifications of their own publicity. Here again we strike the vulgar egotist lode, but, as in the case of a duchess of the screen who finds it impossible to walk into a railroad carriage without making an "entrance," it is practically impossible to say where egotism leaves off and showmanship begins. In both cases there is indicated a large ingredient of exhibitionism, a delight in showing oneself, and there can be no question but that Barnum loved the adulation of the crowd as much as any pretty stenographer who finds herself transformed, largely by the magic he invented, into the shadowy sweetheart of half the hungry world. We have been given a picture of him standing in his carriage in the center of the circus-ring, crying, "I suppose you want to see Mis-ter Barnum. Wel-ll, I'm

Mis-ter Barnum," and between this, and the film star making her entrance, there is no perceptible difference. Some itch of self-love has been satisfied, some pang of hunger stilled, and the public, instead of being damned, as old Commodore Vanderbilt thought was proper, has been convincingly impressed ——as, indeed, it must be: for to the public belongs the glory to grant, and the power, and also the money whose getting is an art.

Admitting Barnum's importance, his immeasurable influence upon the world-civilization in which John Applegate lives, it is still impossible to claim for him a place in the gallery of great Americans——the ideal of money getting, which is but the ideal of millionairedom brought down to the level of ordinary aspiration, is somehow not enough. The artist, however, finding no inspiration in his average American face, might yet be moved to introduce his figure into a larger, more crowded composition——a mural, let us say, that might be called, perhaps, "P. T. Barnum Spreads The Gospel."

The artist must mix his colors for an American palette, vivid and clashing and raw, and, at the focal point of his composition, in the upper center, place the master on a throne. The throne should be a gaudy circus thing of red and gold, resting on a pile of foamy clouds, and Barnum ought to be wearing his ringmaster's costume——the black shiny boots, the scarlet waistcoat, the high silk hat, the buttons of polished brass. One hand, the fingers flexed, rests lightly on his knee: in the other he holds a copy of his autobiography, open to *The Art of Money Getting*——he has just come from reading it aloud. There is a glow of satisfaction on his face, the lines of his mouth tracing a gentle benedictory smile, his head illumined by a burst of light that falls like a golden Biblical ray from the brilliant American sky.

Behind the throne, to the right, Jumbo's head is reared—— the small shrewd eyes, the outspread ears, the great tusks almost embracing the master in their slow majestic curve—— while to the left, flying, Jenny Lind trails the diaphanous drapes of song. Mrs. Tom Thumb sits in a diminutive chair at the master's feet, her husband standing behind her with his right hand on her left shoulder, both wearing their wedding clothes, and on either side of the throne, the beasts of the jungle are ranged——the blunt snout of the hippopotamus, the rhinoceros' ivory horn, the tiger's burning hide, the grinning taunt of the apes, the long delicate neck of the giraffe.

Below these, the tones of their business suits in sober contrast to the brilliant hues above, a host of enraptured disciples. But upon their worshipful faces, repeating in their general averageness the averageness of the master's countenance, a certain sense and hue of tragedy: the puzzled and frustrated bewilderment of those who, having come into possession of a kingly estate, do not quite know how to make themselves respected; who, in the social sphere, have never been able to rise to the concept of service without financial profit; whose blind idealism about work, about success, about the art of money getting, conceals an intense materialism about life.

Then, beneath these, in a chaos of color and design, the various instruments employed in the master's educational program——the radio microphone, the advertising layout, the billboard, the sound-track, the poster, the illuminated sign—— all seeming to plunge through space and explode like meteors above the swarming mass of figures that seethes across the bottom of the canvas, giving the impression of a dark and restless sea. Here the faces are shadowy and indistinct, joined in blank anonymous kinship, one no different from the other ——all save two.

The first of these is John Applegate, puzzled, bemused, trying to make up his mind what kind of electric sweeper he wants to buy, wishing he had money enough to get the one he cannot afford. The other, lost in the crowd, his white hair and pale face giving him a kind of dramatic isolation, is Thomas Jefferson—introduced into the composition, we gather, out of some whim or fancy of the artist. Jefferson also holds a book, the *Notes On Virginia*, open to the passage in which he recorded his belief in the value and importance of education. (*"Every government degenerates when trusted to the rulers of the people alone. The people themselves are its only safe depositories. And to render even them safe, their minds must be improved to a certain degree."*) There is a worried expression on his face, a kind of baffled brooding that further emphasizes his solitary loneliness, and gradually we come to understand that he is wondering, as he looks upon this scene of Barnum's triumph, if he might also be witnessing a threat to a vision and the ruin of a dream. What of the night, watchman, he seems to be asking; what of the storms to come? The dark crowd gives no answer. Barnum, sitting on his throne, smiles and looks serene.

· 7 ·

HENRY ADAMS AND
WILLIAM JENNINGS BRYAN
The American Turns the Century

IN 1893, when Grover Cleveland was in the White House
for his second term, the World's Fair in Chicago was
opened——all the earth's peoples were invited to come
and bear witness to the brawn and bustle of the strapping
young giant of the West.

John Applegate was then only a boy of nine, but memories
of the Fair, to which his father took him on a three-day ex-
cursion, often return with an extraordinary vividness. He
found himself telling Sonny, when Chicago again played host
to the world many years later, that this new and more garish
exposition could in no way compare with the old——there was
nothing, for example, that approached the Court of Honor in
beauty, or the gleaming white Administration Building in
architectural impressiveness. It was the effect of the exposition as a whole, however, rather than the wealth of its separate parts, that made such an indelible impression upon John
Applegate's mind——the majestic colonnades, the graceful
arches, the shimmering domes, the swards of greenery with
their interlacing tracery of quiet lagoons. His nine-year-old
eyes drank the wonder in and, if through the gauze of years
he remembers it as a thing of magic beyond compare, his
lingering appreciation is only slightly greater than was that
of Henry Adams who overcame his misanthrophic antipathy

to most aspects of American life long enough to declare: "As a scenic display, Paris never approached it."

Most of Adams' countrymen felt a similar enthusiasm——throughout the nation there ran a general feeling of exhilarated pride. Millions of Americans, seeing Chicago for the first time, came to realize something of the astonishing saga of the West; the miracle of growth that, in but the span of a single lifetime from 1837 to 1893, had transformed an empty wilderness where wolves howled against the intrusion of scattered trading-posts to a large and thriving city. And there were others who, as they stood before the reproductions of the ships of Columbus' fleet sent to the exhibition by the Queen of Spain, the *Pinta, Niña* and *Santa Maria*, were bound to find their imaginations straying to a consideration of the short but immensely eventful American past——a nation's coming of age.

The American had always been conscious of his own uniqueness, hewing his sense of personality out of the wilderness even as he carved his freedom, but now there was added an awareness of the uniqueness of his country. There was a surge of national self-consciousness, a pride in swift achievement, a conviction of strength and authority and increasing power. The American mind, notoriously distrustful of Europe, suspicious of foreigners and all things foreign, was further confirmed in its own isolationism——an historically conditioned reflex, rather than a moral failing, that was to grow increasingly more stubborn and pronounced.

Ever since the War of 1812, when the British under Packenham were routed by Andrew Jackson at the battle of New Orleans, no real threat had been leveled at American independence from abroad. The intervening years had merely strengthened a sense of national self-sufficiency that first began to develop after the defeat of the French in the fourth French-and-Indian War. There had been the affair of Charlotte and Maximilian in Mexico, and in 1870 rumors began to circulate that a foreign power, thought to be Germany, had designs on the island of San Domingo, but these events barely rippled the surface of American indifference and calm. There were two worlds, the Old and the New, and they shared practically nothing in common. Even the moon, in that era of serene self-immolation, began to take on those peculiarly American attributes it has retained ever since——being, on the banks of the Wabash, a quite different and unquestionably superior moon than the one that shone down upon the banks of the Seine, or the Rhine, or the Volga.

George Washington had vividly impressed the American consciousness with his principle of "no entangling alliances," a statement of isolationist doctrine that both Thomas Jefferson and Andrew Jackson had emphatically reaffirmed, and in that year of the Chicago Fair, as the country neared the presidential campaign of 1896 and the Spanish-American war, the belief that the United States might follow the workings of its own destiny without help or hindrance from abroad was rarely, if ever, questioned or denied. There was even then the belief, more distinctly characteristic of a later isolationism, that Europe was hopelessly stricken with an incurable disease, bled white with hate and endless wars, ground between the millstones of too feckless a way of life and too fatal a way of history. Self-trust passed ever increasingly into self-satisfaction, self-satisfaction into self-love, self-love into doting, and on its great island between the seas a people turned its back upon the world. If there was a hope, and a promise, America contained them both. God was in His Heaven, looking after His favorite people, and all the trials were over.

II

Andrew Carnegie, talkative as ever, voiced in 1893 the large complacency of his time. He compared the era to "high noon, when the blazing sun overhead casts no shadows . . . There is not one shred of privilege to be met with anywhere in all the laws. One man's right is every man's right. The flag is the guarantor and symbol of equality." The time, in sum, was perfect.

There were those who might dispute the perfection of the age——the one million citizens who voted the Populist ticket the year before; the other millions who were part of the rising labor movement described in Samuel Gomper's autobiography——but John Applegate, musing upon his memories of the Chicago Fair and the years that marked his coming to man's estate, would be tempted to agree with the steelmaster. He recalls the world's climate as being warmer then, the conditions of life more fixed and secure, and while he has been driven to the understanding that the years from 1893 to 1914 were twilight years, hung with the threat of unsuspected doom, there yet remains enough of sentiment and nostalgia to put a halo about the time and turn it into his own Golden Age.

Even the Spanish-American War, as he recalls it, was but a cloud quickly devoured by the sun. He now knows, vaguely, that those years saw the growth of the United States into an international power, that the war with Spain was more than a high vaudeville crossed with a scandal of bad beef, crowded with consequences and implications that no man foresaw, but, in terms of his own education, the historic events of that period left him almost untouched. William Jennings Bryan he remembers principally as Clarence Darrow's opponent at the Dayton "monkey trial" in 1925, revolving about a statute passed by a Fundamentalist-dominated Tennessee legislature that made it unlawful to teach "any theory that denies the story of the Divine creation of man as taught in the Bible," *(Listen! Hear the voice of Cotton Mather, drifting on the wind)* and Theodore Roosevelt, who loomed like a giant in the years of his youth, has gradually faded into a ghostly image with big teeth and glasses and a cowboy's hat——"busting" trusts that, as things turned out, managed to survive unbusted and, in true American fashion, went marching on.

But though John Applegate knows it not, or is carelessly indifferent to the knowledge, the old American debate, the prolonged contest between the few and the many over the right to rule, still troubled the deeps of American life. Even less than P. T. Barnum can William Jennings Bryan be ranked as one of John Applegate's important Americans, his total heritage being hardly more than a single phrase, but it was he, "the Tiberius Gracchus of the West," who, in the campaign of 1896, voiced the last challenge of the rapidly disappearing frontier——one of the major conquests over nature the Chicago Fair had been raised to celebrate.

When the Democratic convention met in 1896 to nominate its candidate for the Presidency, William McKinley, largely through the efforts of Mark Hanna, had already been selected as the Republican nominee, and a platform drawn up supporting the gold standard and opposing the coinage of free silver unless by international agreement. The Democrats, divided among themselves, met in an atmosphere of tense excitement. The agrarian radicals of the South and West, determined to impose their will upon the convention, had been busily seeking delegates and so dominated the gathering that the opening prayer contained a special passage of sympathy "for our toiling multitudes, oppressed with burdens too heavy for them to bear."

Contrary to Andrew Carnegie, it was a discontented era,

not a perfect one, and all the efforts of the more conservative Democrats to dam the tide of rebelliousness were swept aside. The moment of climax came when Bryan, then only thirty-six years old, wearing the black string tie and alpaca coat that were to become established as his trademark, flung the challenge into the camp of the plutocracy. Defiantly he recited the roll call of those for whom he spoke——the workman, the country merchant, the small town lawyer, the miner, the farmer——and summoned them with religious zeal to rally about the silver banner that floated above his head.

"It is for these we speak," he cried. "We do not come as aggressors. Ours is not a war of conquest. We are fighting in defense of our homes, our families and our posterity. We have petitioned and our petitions have been scorned. We have entreated and our entreaties have been disregarded. We have begged and they have mocked when calamity came. We beg no longer; we entreat no more; we petition no more. We defy them. We shall answer their demands for a gold standard by saying to them: You shall not press down upon the brow of labor this crown of thorns. You shall not crucify mankind upon a cross of gold."

Emily Applegate, coming upon this passage in one of her history books, finds it hard to understand what the excitement was all about. The various issues central to the campaign of 1896——that of free silver in particular——seem incredibly outmoded and old hat. And the full-blown style of the Boy Orator of the Platte, ("A river six inches deep and six inches wide at the mouth," one of his critics said) serves chiefly to confirm her impression that he belonged to the spread-eagle school of public speakers——those who kept the national bird so constantly on wing, according to the backwoods humorists, that its passing shadow wore a two-foot trail down the Mississippi Valley. But difficult though it may be for Emily to comprehend the alarm, even the terror, Bryan's nomination aroused, causing Edwin Lawrence Godkin, the founder of *The Nation*, to write of the Democratic convention that selected him: "Beside them the Populists are lamblike, and the socialists suckling doves. The country has watched their mad proceedings with disgust and shuddering, only impatient for the coming of November to stamp out them and their incendiary doctrines"——despite the apparent lack of reason for such hysterical outcries as this, the fact is that in the election of 1896 the country was called upon to take part in the most sharply defined struggle of economic groups since the first campaign of Lincoln.

The westward march of Empire had ended. Free land was giving out and it was becoming increasingly more apparent that other natural resources were equally limited. Farmers already in possession of land were forced to sell their produce at ruinous prices on a glutted market—"Raise less corn and more hell," the cry was raised in Kansas. Trusts and monopolies had arisen, the growing industrialism had been accompanied by the growth of an angry labor movement whose foremost champion was John P. Altgeld, "The Flaming Eagle" of Illinois, and both the Populist and Greenback movements had been broken by defeat. Bryan's proposed solution to the troubles of the era, his mystic ratio of sixteen to one, is now clearly seen as an economic panacea no more valid than Huey P. Long's "Share the Wealth" program. Somewhat less apparent is the fact that, born though it may have been out of a great ignorance about money, Bryan's hope in silver contained the aspirations of a nobler, more idealistic hope.

The wilderness was no longer the wilderness——the land going, the game going, the forests going——and with the wilderness had passed the wilderness voices. There was no Jefferson, no Jackson, no Lincoln. Some intangible quality had gone forever from American life——the quality, perhaps, lent by men who knew the lessons of nature before they came to the lessons of books—but still, somewhere in Bryan's oratory of that year, rising above the rhetoric, the cracked voice, the distillery reek that came from his bizarre habit of cooling his neck and arms with gin, somewhere there might be heard a last defiant shouting of the old, the familiar, the frontier challenge—the people, not the elect, have the right to rule!

The cry was to be raised again, and yet again, but now for the last time it was threaded with the experience and education of the geographical frontier. And whatever the future's shape, whatever its cast or content, it was inevitably destined to be different from the past. The long, hard labor was over: a continent had been won. The frontier, now, as the wheel of years turned upon the great axle of the century, was the illimitable frontier of time.

III

In the summer of 1896 the aging Henry Adams was once again in Paris. The old *malaise* was upon him, the tired disillusion, and his letters of the period are full of the weary world-sickness he came in the end almost to enjoy. During the early part of August he visited Chartres, spending a Sunday afternoon with the service and the glass, and upon his return to Paris he wrote his old friend, Elizabeth Cameron:

> In my sublimated fancy, the combination of the glass and the Gothic is the highest ideal ever yet reached by man; higher than the Mosaics and Byzantine of Ravenna, which was itself higher, as a religious conception, than the temples of the Greeks or Egyptians. Our age is too thoroughly brutalized to approach or understand any of these creations of an imagination which is dead. I am myself somewhat like a monkey looking through a telescope at the stars; but I can see at least that it must have been great.

There is a wrongness, however, (a wrongness that Adams

himself often fell into: or was it a pose?) in emphasizing too strongly the anachronistic quality of his imagination. Disillusioned he was, harshly contemptuous of the commercial ideals of his generation, but, at the same time, he never permitted his gaze, no matter how enraptured by the glories of Chartres or Mont Saint-Michel, to stray very far from the contemporary scene. In the same letter wherein he describes himself as a monkey looking through a telescope, he goes on to say:

> Yesterday I read through a whole week of American papers. Frankly my impression was that Bryan could not destroy anything worth preserving, if he makes a clean sweep of all we have. Always, hitherto, I have hated revolutions, not so much on account of the revolutions as on account of the subsequent reaction; but at last I am getting to think that rot and moral atrophy are worse than revolution or reaction.
>
> Paris has had no end of revolutions. Great moats of blood separate everybody from everybody's neighbor. Yet Paris is full of a dozen interests and vigorous influences which exist chiefly because of their mutual animosities, while we have absolutely nothing in our minds except whether we had best make our living by gold or silver.
>
> No doubt Bryan's success would mean chaos, and general ruin for a time, and probably a great breach with Europe. Well! Like Rochefort, I feel as though it were time to say to the public about their duties: *Peuple américain, est-ce que décidément tu ne trouves pas qu'en voilà assez!* If we allow the crushing intellectual imbecility of McKinley and his Ohio-Pennsylvania following to master us completely, you know the type that must survive. *Décidément je trouve déjà qu'en voilà plus qu'assez!* I am already stifled by it; what will happen when it alone exists in America! Still believing that McKinley will certainly win, I trust that, like most such men and such régimes, he will create more hostility than revolution itself. But at any rate all my sympathies and all my best

wishes are for his opponent, and the larger his support, the better I will be pleased.

The revolt of Henry Adams, if revolt it may be called, was similar to that of Henry James——a protest against the ideals of millionairedom and Barnum's art of money getting. "If," wrote Adams, "there is such a thing in America as an earnest impulse, an energy or a thought outside of dollars and cents, I should like to see it before total imbecility sets in." Between James and Adams, however, the points of opposition are more striking than those of similarity——for, while James made a notable effort to oppose the ideals of millionairedom with those of art, Adams permitted himself to sink deeper and deeper into the querulous misanthrophy which, in the end, was to become little more than the bored negation of a spoiled and self-indulgent snob.

"If you asked me to find out five hundred persons in the world you would like to give the volume," he wrote his brother Brooks just before the publication of *Mont Saint-Michel and Chartres*," I could only say that, as far as you and I know, five hundred do not exist—nor half that number——nor a quarter of it.

" 'As far as you and I know,' and I suspect we know of everybody worth knowing. Thousands of people exist who think they want to read. Barring a few Jews, they are incapable of reading fifty consecutive pages, or of following the thought if they did. I never yet heard of ten men who had ever read my history and never one who had read Hay's *Lincoln* . . .

Of course there are several hundred thousand persons in Boston and out of it, who are lecture-goers and frequent libraries; and there are one or two million young women who read poetry in Browning clubs, and mostly come to Paris to study art when they can. I imagine that neither you nor I care much to be admired by these, but in any case they will admire us the more at secondhand.

We need not lift a finger to reach that class, who are quite passive, and mere reed-pods of receptivity."

It is not surprising, therefore, with this blight of bitterness and snobbism upon him, that when he published his book he issued it in a private edition limited to one hundred copies. What had he, who saw in the combination of glass and Gothic the highest ideal ever reached by man, to say to the America of Andrew Carnegie and Pierpont Morgan; to the dilletante young women who read Browning in poetry clubs and studied art in Paris; to those incapable of reading fifty pages? Nothing, he gave the answer——nothing at all.

The deepest impression left by his letters, however, is that he had much to say——that, for whatever the reason, one of the ablest and most far-reaching minds of its generation was permitted to go to waste. Adams was a true world-citizen, beside whom Henry James seems almost provincial at times, and during that era of unbridled nationalistic pride, when a bustling and self-confident America was divorcing itself from the rest of the world, he looked at the global complex and saw, among the many other things that make his correspondence an invaluable guide to the period, traces of the road that would lead, in time, to the tomb of the unknown soldier. To his brother Brooks he wrote:

As far as I can see, the various forces are now fairly well defined. The disruption of '93 has definitely rearranged society and we need not fret about new disturbances because we cannot any longer increase or diminish the forces. That another shock and disruption will come, and come soon, everyone admits——not that the admission proves anything. What form it will take is another matter. In my opinion, the center of readjustment, if readjustment it is to be, lies in Germany, not in Russia or in us. For the last generation, since 1865, Germany has been the greatly disturbing element of the world, and until its expansive force is decidedly exhausted, I can see neither political nor economical equilibrium possible.

In another letter, written in the autumn of 1897 to the English diplomat, Cecil Spring Rice, he continues this train of thought:

> Do you know the kinetic theory of gases? Anyway, Germany is and always has been a remarkably apt illustration of Maxwell's conception of 'sorting demons.' By bumping against all its neighbors, and being bumped in turn, it gets and gives at last a common motion which is, and of necessity must be, a vortex or cycle. It can't get anywhere except round a circle and return on itself. It has done so since the time of Varus and his legions . . .

In 1898, when the Spanish-American war broke out, Adams was in Athens. "My mind," he wrote, "wanders terribly fast between Salamis, where Xerxes is before my eyes, and Key West where our ships are waiting orders. The moment is perhaps a turning point in history; in any case it can hardly fail to fix the lines of a new concentration, and to throw open an immense new field of difficulties. The world is abjectly helpless. It is running a race to nowhere. Slowly and painfully our people are waking up to the new world they are to live in."

There is a certain esthetic correctness in Adams's remoteness from America at a time when the nation was marching off to war. Sitting on the platform of the Pnyx, clambering across the fields at Phaleron and Eleusis, brooding on past and present and future——this is what we "expect" of this arch-intellectual, telling his beads of private thought alone and above the battle. Yet was he any more remote from the conflict, except in terms of geography, than most of his countrymen——did he not, from his ivory Grecian tower, see its meaning more clearly? America was agitated, to be sure, by all the noise and excitement of war——the balls, the parades, the flags flying, the bands playing *Waltz Me Around, Willie* and *There'll Be A Hot Time In The Old Town Tonight*——but the war itself was over too quickly, too successfully, ever to get beyond the *opera bouffe* stage.

Perhaps, as Adams believed when he wrote from Athens, the people of America were slowly and painfully waking up to the new world in which they were to live. But, in 1900, when he had again taken up residence in the Washington that both fascinated and repelled him, he could nowhere discover the dawn. The country, he reported, was

> full of swagger and satisfaction. The change since 1893 is startling. A war or two seems a matter of entire indifference. Grumblers have to scold in private, for they get nothing but chaff in reply. As for money, it seems to lie about loose, for no one confesses to want of it. Even I, who own infinity, open my eyes at the way we sling things about, and the calm acceptance of the new scale . . . There is no longer the smallest sense of responsibility for consequences. Fifty years ago, we all expected to break our necks at half the speed, but now we look forward to doubling it without a qualm . . .

Full of swagger and satisfaction——it was in this mood that the nation faced the opening of the new century. The war had served merely to intensify the general conviction of American superiority, to deepen the feeling of national pride. Perhaps, as has become ritualized to say, the war with Spain had meant largely the triumph of William Randolph Hearst ——"a blackguard boy with several million dollars at his disposal," Godkin of *The Nation* called him. Yet behind the figure of the Lord of San Simeon, whose incredible California palace was but the most outrageous example of a great glut of castles that arose across the land, leaving hardly an American community without a gloomy pile destined eventually to become known as somebody or other's "folly," whose rapacious pillaging of the trash and treasure of Europe was merely one millionaire's indulgence in a highly popular sport, (Did not one of Hearst's contemporaries, Joseph Leiter, offer to buy the Great Wall of China?), whose untrammelled individualism was but an extravagant acting-out of the generally accepted theory, stated most notably by William Graham Sumner of Yale, that individualism (i.e. *laissez faire*) was the mainspring of civilization——behind the figure of Hearst triumphant there stood a triumphant people.

"We will cover the ocean with our merchant marine," Albert J. Beveridge cried out during a speech that sought to endow imperialism with the same supernatural sanction the early Puritans found implicit in success. "We will build a navy to the measure of our greatness. Great colonies governing themselves, flying our flag and trading with us, will grow about our posts of trade. Our institutions will follow our flag on the wings of our commerce. And American law, American order, American civilization, and the American flag will plant themselves on shores hitherto bloody and benighted, but by those agencies of God henceforth to be made beautiful and bright."

Full of swagger and satisfaction——how well had Adams caught the spirit of the time. Later voices would rise in protest——socialists like Jack London and Upton Sinclair, the army of muckrakers led by Lincoln Steffens, academic rebels like Thornstein Veblen, political insurgents like Robert M. LaFollette——but, as the people of the nation stood on the threshold of a brand-new century, most of them would have been in general agreement with Beveridge that American seapower, American law, American institutions and the American flag were truly agencies of a superior civilization and not improbably of God.

IV

By using the method of historical liturgy——the method, that is, which selects certain events for particular emphasis or celebration——it may be argued that the period from 1898 to 1914 saw the end of American "isolationism" rather than its firm entrenchment. With beguiling simplicity, the terms of this argument run as follows: The war of 1898 forced the United States to assume responsibilities, not only in the Caribbean, but as far away as the Philippines. The dash of the battleship *Oregon* from San Francisco around the Horn, in order to participate in the battle of Manila, dramatically demonstrated the need of a canal across the Panama Isthmus ——the canal, in turn, made plain the necessity of a "two-ocean" navy. Beyond this, concludes the argument, the United States had recognized its vital interest in the peace of Asia by participating in the settlement of the Russo-Japanese war, and in the peace of Europe by its representation at the Algeciras conference.*

But what is here overlooked, or sacrificed to the demands of neatness, is that it is not impossible for internationalism and isolationism to walk hand in hand——that even so narrow a strip of water as the English channel is wide enough to help create a certain insularity of thought and temperament; that,

---

* France, in 1904, made certain agreements with England and Spain leading to an increase of her influence in Morocco. Germany, feeling she had been rebuffed, demanded a conference of the signatories of an earlier agreement concerning Morocco negotiated at Madrid in 1880. To the United States, a signatory of the 1880 agreement, Germany appealed for an extension of the "open-door" policy to include Morocco. President Theodore Roosevelt, seeking a peaceful solution, persuaded the contending nations to attend a conference at Algeciras, Spain, in 1906. The attitude of Germany, however, was so uncompromising that Roosevelt threw his influence to the side of France which won a privileged position in Morocco. The resulting treaty was ratified by the United States Senate, but a formal declaration was made that the action was taken only to protect American interests and should not be construed as an abandonment of a non-intervention policy toward Europe.

more specifically, while the annexation of the islands in the
Pacific may have weakened the geographic foundation of
American isolationism it did not undermine its popularity, nor
altar the ingrained belief, revealed as early as 1775-76 when
the Continental Congress hesitated to enter into an alliance
with France, that in the continental insularity of the United
States there was contained the promise of a unique destiny,
separate and detached from that of the rest of the world.
The native suspicion of Europe had in no way been diminished——had, if anything, been deepened by the Boer War
——and along with the suspicion there ran a profession of contempt. Thus, when the German Emperor on January 1, 1900,
announced his intention of building up the German army to
parity with the German navy, ushering in the new century
with as noisy a piece of symbolism as history records, it was
either ignored or put down as another example of European
incorrigibility. Before the assembled officers of the Berlin garrison the Kaiser said:

> The first day of the new century sees our army——in
> other words, our people——in arms, gathered around
> their standards, kneeling before the Lord of Hosts . . .
> Even as my grandfather labored for his army, so will I,
> in like manner, carry on and carry through the work of
> reorganizing my navy in order that it may be justified in
> standing by the side of my land-forces and that by it the
> German Empire may also be in a position to win the place
> which it has not yet attained. With the two united, I hope
> to be enabled, with a firm trust in the guidance of God,
> to prove the truth of the saying of Frederick William the
> First: "When one in this world wants to decide some-
> thing with the pen he does not do it unless supported by
> the strength of the sword."

Many persons doubtless read the speech with grave concern,
Henry Adams certainly among them, he finding in it further

evidence that the kinetic theory of gases had social and political application, that once again Germany was "bumping
against all its neighbors," but the more general view was
summed up by an editorial writer for *The New York World*:

"If Emperor William had sought to wear a costume ap-
propriate to the speech he made at Berlin yesterday, the
latest possible style he could have adopted would have been
a suit of early mediaeval armor . . . He and his pose are
melancholy reminders of a past whose lessons have been all
too imperfectly learned."

What these lessons were the writer did not trouble to say.
But America, the implication ran, had taken them seriously to
heart—rejecting, in the process of her education, all such Old
World folly. The possible effect that the creation of a larger
German navy might have upon America was nowhere publicly considered. Nor, in popular opinion, could it have any.
The great island—immense, unique, immune—still lay bas-
tioned by the seas. Whatever shocks might quake the earth
of Europe, in whatever skies the storm might rage, here at
home the island earth would remain unshaken, the island sky
serene. The wisdom of the Almighty, in placing the waters
of the earth where He did, had never seemed more profound.

Grateful for the continental insularity of the United States,
looking upon it as a gift handed down from above, the turn-
of-the century American might justify his complacency with
verse from Goethe and celebration from Hegel. In 1827,
moved to signalize the escape of America from the tyrannies
of Europe, Goethe had written:

> Amerika, du hast es besser
> Als unser Kontinent, der alte,
> Du hast keine verfallene Schlösser
> Und keine Basalte.

Dich stört nicht im Innern
Zu lebendiger Zeit
Unnützes Erinnern
Und vergeblicher Streit.*

Hegel, whose theory of the state as the only absolute reality
had been interestingly paralleled in part by John Calhoun of
South Carolina, was also prompted to praise America. In his
Philosophy of History he called it "the land of the future
where, in the ages that lie before us, the burden of the
World's History shall reveal itself . . . the land of desire for
all those who are weary of the historical lumber-room of old
Europe."

America was not so highly regarded by most other Europeans, Matthew Arnold summing up the general view by calling it "uninteresting" and Sigmund Freud the extreme one by
regretting its discovery as "a terrible mistake," but even these
critics agreed that the new world had nothing in common
with the old. With so many voices saying so, and with the
map of the earth's surface to back them up, the American had
no more reason to dispute the geographic and cultural uniqueness of the United States than to deny its temperate climate.
And if this implied a rejection of Europe, a more intense interest in the affairs of Main Street than the broad highways
of the world, he might reply that he was acting on the advice of Europe's most advanced and intelligent minds. Even
Napoleon, Hegel reminded him, was said to have complained,
"Cette vieille Europe m'ennuie."

----

* America, you have it better
Than our old continent,
You have no ruins
No tormented stones.

No futile memories
Or vain strife
Vex thy inner spirit
In this living hour.

The American, then, coming into the Twentieth Century, could consider himself guilty of no moral failing in feeling similarly bored. Europe was the past, America the future. As a citizen of that future, inhabiting "the land of desire" he subscribed to its promise much as he might have subscribed to stock in a gold mine——rashly, perhaps, but hopeful and unafraid.

·8·

THEODORE ROOSEVELT FEELS FIT
AS A BULL MOOSE
The American As Progressive

AT THE END of the Spanish-American War, when all
America was singing Theodore Roosevelt's theme song,
There'll Be a Hot Time In the Old Town Tonight,
all England was singing the slightly more abandoned non-
sense of *Ta-ra-ra-ra-boom-de-ay*, the theme song of *fin de
siècle*. "It affected the country like an epidemic," Holbrook
Jackson wrote in *The Eighteen Nineties*, discovering in it
"the absurd *ça ira* of a generation that was bent on kicking
over the traces," much as later social historians were to find an
equally absurd *ça ira* in the no less nonsensical chorus of *Jada*,
which helped serve notice that the post-war Jazz Age had arrived.

Between the England of *fin de siècle*, of Oscar Wilde and
Aubrey Beardsley, of Max Beerbohm and George Bernard
Shaw, of Dandyism and *The Yellow Book*—between this
England and bustling, materialistic, turn-of-the-century
America, John Applegate would find little in common. A faint
aura of decadence still hangs over *Ta-ra-ra-ra-boom-de-ay*,
suggesting the foamy petticoats and gartered thighs of the
can-can, while *There'll Be a Hot Time* has come to take on
all the worth and respectability of an old-fashioned Fourth of
July picnic. But it may have been more than coincidence that
brought these two songs to popularity at the same time: both
may have been different reflections of a relatively similar tem-

per and mood. For if *fin de siècle* was at once a swan song and a death-bed repentance, as has been said, the early 1900's in America saw more than the passing of one century and the beginning of another——a cycle of change was in motion, along with a cycle of time.

"The disposition of the times is curiously confused," wrote Max Nordau, "a compound of feverish restlessness and blunted discouragement, of fearful presage and hangdog renunciation. The prevalent feeling is that of imminent perdition and extinction. *Fin de siècle* is both a confession and a complaint. The old Northern faith contained the fearsome doctrine of the Dusk of the Gods. In our days there have arisen in more highly developed minds vague qualms of the Dusk of Nations, in which all suns and all stars are gradually waning, and mankind with all its institutions is perishing in the midst of a dying world."

John Applegate, aware though he is that the world of the early 1900's was perhaps less securely fastened to its moorings than it seemed, would not subscribe to such a pessimistic summing-up as this. The time, as he recalls it, was one of bustle and enterprise, full of the swaggering self-confidence Henry Adams had noticed, when the world, instead of being threatened with extinction, seemed fated to move onward and upward on prosperity's unceasing curve. Deeply conscious of change, finding the world he lives in scarcely recognizable as the world of his youth, he charges such change to the War of 1914-18. It was the War, he imagines, and the generation that was young when the War began, that destroyed one America and produced another. But correct though he is about the War, and while the generation that grew up during the War was indeed the seed-carrier of much significant change, outdoing any of its predecessors in its irreverence of tribal gods, the roots of change go back to the early years of the century and the decade that went before.

Ideas and conventions which had long been regarded as permanent were being challenged years before the War began. Movements and enthusiasms generally associated with The Younger Generation, such as psychoanalysis and the theory of economic determinism, were already noticeable as early as 1910. Skirts and the divorce rate began to go up, family prayers and the chaperon began to disappear, codes that had hardened into something like the authority of religious concepts began to be swept aside. But this drift in human relations and the current of ideas, interesting thought it was, had a greater importance in that it was the result of a deeper and more revolutionary drift in American life.

At the turn of the century, just before the assassination of McKinley brought Theodore Roosevelt and his athletic way of living into the White House, the dinosaurian capitalists whose principal devotion was to Barnum's art of money getting had no reason to suppose that the bright sun of the Gilded Age would ever pass from the sky. But other factors than they were at work. The rebellious farmers who had gone down to defeat with Bryan in 1896 were growing more restive, the increasing army of industrial workers was moving toward a closer solidarity, the very vitality of capitalist ambition itself contributed to the relentless drift. Instead of being the serene era of John Applegate's imagination, it was a time of ferment and dissatisfaction, of technological and intellectual discovery, of challenge and counter-challenge. The contributions of science, now beginning to reach into every home, permitted no man to escape the realization he was living in an age of change. The automobile arrived, the motion picture, the electric light, the flying-machine. Even more important than these fruits of science, however, was the impact of newly discovered scientific laws upon speculative thought.

The long drama of the conflict between science and religion in America, and its effect upon American thought, is too ramified and complicated to be told here. It is perhaps enough to say, however, that by the end of the Nineteenth Century the Calvinistic Puritanism of New England had long since broken down. Even where it kept its intolerance, or ran off into those evangelical sects that the Puritans would have despised, it lost its metaphysical zeal. Pragmatic and materialistic thinking had been given a great stimulus by the Industrial Revolution, and now a further impetus was provided by Darwinian evolution, historical geology, and the new discoveries in chemistry and physics. The Scriptures were examined in the light of "higher criticism," religious experience was brought down to the level of other mental phenomena by physiological psychology, improvement of the individual and society by means of science and sociology displaced the earlier concern with theology and religion. A whole new school of political and social criticism came into being, proud of its scientific approach, challenging intellectual patterns that had gone unquestioned since the days of the covered wagon.

Almost overnight, it seemed, with the coming of the Industrial Revolution, the nation had entered upon an immense new field of difficulties. The cry that disturbed the plutocratic *élite* was still the frontier challenge——the people, not the elect, have the right to rule——but now the frontier was no more. Free land had given out. The plowshare of industrialism, breaking ground for the factories, seemed also to have turned under the unlimited promise once inherent in the vast continental domain. The pattern of decentralization that for over a hundred years had scattered men across the face of a continent now became a pattern of concentration. The frontier turned into the frontier of the city street.

The psychology of the nation, along with its appearance, began to change. The old voices of agrarian affirmation were lost in urban confessions of defeat. The almost spontaneous democracy of the backwoods, the democracy that was free before it was independent, that had hewn its sense of freedom out of the wilderness and implanted the idea of liberty in the American mind——this great crucible of hope and experience was weighed in the scales of economic determinism and found wanting. The drift toward capitalistic plutocracy, it was held, was most clearly seen as the inevitable flowering of the founding fathers' chief intent. The advance guard, claiming to speak in the name of scientific realism, closed the doors of democracy and invited the nation to embark on a new and non-democratic future. The promise of American life, in some men's minds, had run out to nothing.

Such disillusionment, in time, would come to seem more than a little extreme. For despite all the errors and inadequacies that could be charged to the American system, regardless of the fact that the industrial capitalists constituted the hard core of the ruling class, predatory in its instincts and undemocratic in its impulses, there yet remained the unmistakable evidence, large as the continent itself, that during the years of its existence the American system had provided a larger and more durable base for political freedom, and brought about a wider distribution of this world's goods, than any ever devised. The view put forward by the more advanced progressive thinkers that democracy had failed (just as it would be put forward by later progressive thinkers in the 1930's) would seem to be more indicative of a narrowness of vision than a triumph of realistic thinking. The value of the contribution made by the progressive intellectuals can hardly be overestimated, for it represented the first major critical appraisal of the American system since the dialectic of John Calhoun, but even so confirmed a progressive as Vernon Louis Parrington would eventually come to question if the past had been altogether correctly read.

Seeking a solution to the problem of plutocracy, faced with the fact that monopoly capitalism had gained control of the machinery of government, the progressive intellectuals turned for explanation to the American past, reexamining it in the light of the theory of economic determinism. Here at last was the magic talisman: doors long bolted must now swing open. Not only could the mists of the past be penetrated, but the palm of the future read as well. Prophecy peeped from behind the curtains of the fortune-teller's booth and made ready to enter political science. More important than that, however, as Parrington wrote, was the fact that liberalism "was convinced that somehow economic determinism would turn out to be a fairy godmother to the proletariat and that from the imperious drift of industrial expansion must eventually issue social justice."

We are now able to see, with the clarity of hindsight, that it was not so simple: that these various triumphs of realistic thinking were not without their own content of wishful thinking. Other than this placing of too much trust in the theory of economic determinism, however, two further mistakes on the part of the progressive intellectuals suggest themselves——a rejection, along with the myths and cobwebs of the past, of that body of beliefs, traditions and attitudes which are fairly described as the ethic of American democracy, and a failure to understand that democracy as a form of government depends, in large part, upon the competing interplay of the social forces contained within the structural framework of the democratic state.

John Applegate, coming upon something entitled *The Structural Nature of the Democratic State*, would probably find his attention so aroused as to make him turn it to the baseball scores. In the way he takes his social system for granted, confusing the meaning of politics with the results of local elections, he sometimes seems like a walking denial of

Aristotle's maxim that man is a political animal. Nevertheless, in spite of this indifference, Croce's observation that politics is part of the inner man still remains. This is why the structural nature of the democratic state, which the turn-of-the-century progressive thinkers would seem to have partially misinterpreted, is important to John Applegate whether he realizes it or not.

A democratic state * does not come about, as should be obvious but often is not, simply because of some magic contained in the word democracy. Before such a state can come into being, or successfully maintain itself, it would appear that two essential conditions must prevail—(1) There must be, on the part of the people, a general emotional or ethical preference for democracy over any other form of government, and (2) The state must be composed of a number of relatively independent social forces, bearing more or less arrangement to the state as the atom to the molecule, with no single one of them so powerful as to destroy, absorb or make ineffective the others. Should any such one force attain to this degree of power—capital or labor, the army or the church, the *élite* or the masses—democracy is then destroyed or stands in danger of destruction.

But no less important than the structural nature of the democratic state is the democratic ethic, or, if this seems too lofty a word, the democratic emotion. John Applegate may not know what democracy is, but he knows how he feels about democracy. Emotion is here important as knowledge. And it is this, the ethic or emotion of democracy, that the economic determinists, past and present, have preferred to ignore. Every state, to some degree, is a reflection of the psychology of the

---

* The democratic state is here taken to be one based on popular sovereignty, one that provides full expression for that political opposition without which no democracy is possible, and one in which the democratic privileges that are traditionally associated with the Bill of Rights are recognized.

men and women who live in it. If such men and women are not psychologically disposed toward democracy (as in Germany), or have lost faith in it (as in France just before the outbreak of the War of 1914-18) the structural conditions necessary for the maintenance of the democratic state cannot alone guarantee democracy. If, on the other hand, such a psychological disposition is present (as in America during Colonial times) men and women will continue to struggle for democracy no matter what the cost.

The seminal question put by the early Twentieth Century progressive intellectuals, to which all others were largely auxiliary, was one of enormous and baffling complexity. What they were asking, each in his own way, was *Is democracy possible?* A few, turning to what seemed the brighter promise of socialism, just as many of the intellectuals of the 1930's were to turn to communism, replied in the negative. Others, more hopeful, thought that an approach to the answer lay in the strengthening of the authority of the state.

The state, they felt, having in effect lost its sovereignty to economics, must now reassert that sovereignty and discipline economics for the common good. But here, too, their ambitions would appear worthier than their thinking: the problem of power was ignored——the fact that even in a highly decentralized state power tends to be consolidated in a few hands, and that, in a highly centralized one, Michels' "iron law of oligarchy" may operate without interference. Into the channel of most progressive thinking went everything but a realistic political understanding——good-will, affection for the underdog, an imagined escaped from the treacherous pitfalls of romanticism, anger with the sins and follies of the plutocratic *élite*. Fight the good fight and the good shall triumph: show men the way and men shall follow: increase the authority of the state and the state shall operate for the good of all.

That in this concept of the state——centralized, powerful, disciplinary——they were jettisoning one of Jefferson's cardinal principles, is of only incidental consequence. More significant is the fact that in less than twenty-five years after the fruition of progressive hopes in the election of 1912, when Theodore Roosevelt stood at Armageddon and the dawn of Woodrow Wilson's New Freedom broke across the land, the state itself, by becoming totalitarian in many countries and increasingly authoritarian in others, was to become the main enemy of democracy and invest the question *Is democracy possible?* with new and somber meaning.

Even John Applegate, caught in the currents of world revolution, would have to pause and wonder. In the first years of the Twentieth Century, however, with Theodore Roosevelt in the White House, the idea of world revolution seemed but the distorted nightmare of a madman's dream. The noise in the air was loud enough to be mistaken for the breaking of nations, but it came from the bustings of trusts——that and the beginnings of jazz.

II

The progressive movement, in John Applegate's imagination, is summed up in the character and personality of Theodore Roosevelt. There is reason enough for this, for in the campaign of 1912 Roosevelt gave progressivism the best dramatization of its rather confused career, but there may also be detected some of the irony that seems to be a special fondness of history. Roosevelt was a force in his time, and lent the rebellious elements of his day the color and energy of a flamboyant leadership, but he remains in the American mind for reasons that have little or nothing to do with progressivism.

One of the secondary Americans, properly belonging in the lesser hierarchy reserved for such figures as William Jennings Bryan, the hero of San Juan Hill escaped Bryan's fate largely because he was that hero, became President, shot lions and tigers, and because the ultimate tragedy of his life, which came when Woodrow Wilson would not grant him permission to serve in the War of 1914-18, is a tragedy only by special definition, with none of the burlesque overtones that marked the Dayton monkey-trial.

In the historical balance, however, the scales are nearly equal——Bryan's Democratic populism against Roosevelt's Republican progressivism; the Great Commoner against the Rough Rider; the cross of gold against the big stick. Both were actors, both were gifted with the quality of leadership, both led broad popular movements against entrenched privilege——and both failed. That Roosevelt's failure is never recalled by most Americans, while that of Bryan is attached like a stigma to his memory, is also traceable to the Dayton monkey-trial. Roosevelt, whose greatness was attributed by one admirer to his understanding of the "psychology of the mutt," never permitted himself to be made ridiculous: Bryan, in his insistence that Eve was indeed created from Adam's rib, was too sincere to be that fortunate. The portrait of Bryan that most Americans remember is the one done in mercury by H. L. Mencken. The image of Roosevelt is the one created by himself.

It is this, the way in which whatever issues he happened to represent were submerged in his own personality, that makes him one of the guideposts to the present century. With Roosevelt there is marked the beginning of Twentieth-Century personalism in American government. There had been leaders in America before, and the history of Europe may be written in terms of personal leadership, but during the past in America there had always been a program, or at least a fairly definite attitude toward a program, associated with the man. In the election of 1800, when the victory of Jefferson and his Democratic-Republicans blocked the dangerous monarchial trends of the Federalists, men voted for Jefferson because he was Jefferson, "The People's Friend." Along with these emotional ballots, however, they cast their votes for what he represented. Those who went down with his opponent did likewise.

Daniel Webster, in a later era, was bluntly specific on the point. "If you approve my principles, elect me," he said. "If you disapprove, reject me." And in the famous contest of Lincoln and Douglas, one of the most dramatic clashes of personality in American life, there was also a debate of principles. Lincoln would not have had it otherwise.

After the coming of the Industrial Revolution, however, and the growth of mass democracy accompanied by an increasing ambiguity in political platforms, this stressing of principles tends to disappear. The first signs of modern personalism in government begin to be apparent with the election of General U. S. Grant. In the career of Theodore Roosevelt it takes on the form that characterizes it as one of the distinguishing features of the Twentieth Century. Roosevelt came to the Presidency by a combination of accidents, the ambitions of Mark Hanna and the trajectory of an assassin's bullet happening to coincide at a particular moment in time, but for the rest of his political career he was to run on a platform that had been reduced to the strict simplicity of two initials: T.R. With him, more emphatically than at any time in the past, the American government came to be symbolized by an individual——just as it would later come to be even more notably symbolized by another Roosevelt in an era when the English system was personalized by Winston Churchill, and Stalin, Hitler and Mussolini gave the color and dominance of their own characters to the dictatorships over which they ruled.

On the subject of heroes, and hero-worship, Thomas Carlyle has had much to say. Nor can it be doubted, momentarily passing over some of the objections to his thesis, that the great movements in history have all been marked by the leadership of arresting and unique men. Philip and Alexander in Greece, Julius Caesar in Rome, Napoleon in France, Peter the Great in Russia, Queen Elizabeth in England——the weight of evidence is incontrovertible. But any extreme emphasis upon the principle of leadership, as in Carlyle's idea of the hero, tends to ignore the economic and political drives that lie in the social background. It is hardly likely that Carlyle's idol, Oliver Cromwell, could have come to power if the various forces that made for the Reformation had not already been unleashed. It is just as unlikely that Lenin, the outstanding leader of the early part of the Twentieth Century, could have engineered the Bolshevik Revolution if the armies of the Czar had not been defeated in the War of 1914-18. The theory of individualistic determinism is no less limited than the one that stresses the economic motive to the exclusion of everything else. History, if it has any lessons at all, teaches us that it is multiple-causationist.

It is not enough to say, consequently, that with Theodore Roosevelt there is marked the beginning of Twentieth-Century personalism in American government. There must be added that his arrival on the scene happened to correspond with a period of widespread popular unrest and that in him the voices of unrest found their ideal mouthpiece. If Theodore Roosevelt understood the psychology of the mutt, the mutt found a reflection of his own psychology in that of Theodore Roosevelt. This wedding of understanding and reflection seems essential to the principle of leadership, in democracies as well as in dictatorships.

Distressing though it may be for those whom William James christened the "tender-minded" to think so, it is not unlikely that almost everything that happens in modern politics is eventually based on instincts and emotions. The sum total of these instincts and emotions, in moments of inflammation, make up that herd-instinct or mass-drunkenness that sometimes takes possession of whole peoples. But mass-drunkenness, of itself, cannot be a prime mover in politics because, as Bertrand Russell has said, it cannot determine what the final action of the mass will be. This was proved during the early days of the Russian Revolution. It is here that leadership comes into play. But neither can leadership of itself determine the final result in politics. There is always an interplay of forces. The mass influences leadership, leadership influences the mass. It is only when the articulated ambitions of the former begin to coincide with the unarticulated ambitions of the latter that some kind of decision is reached. The will of Lenin plainly did not represent the whole will of the Russian people. It was representative of enough of their will, however, to make possible the necessary identification. The same thing may be said of Hitler in his relation to the people of Germany.

This is why the arguments of those critics who quarrel with Theodore Roosevelt for not setting the nation on a more revolutionary path fall of their own lack of weight. If revolution was what the country wanted, instead of reform, it could have followed the Socialist, Eugene V. Debs: or, if not Debs, the more truly progressive Robert M. La Follette. The progressive movement was not directed against the American system, with its promise of personal success, but against the monopolistic combines which threatened to nullify that promise. It was the middle-class belief (which in the United States may be considered almost synonymous with the general belief) in the Puritan verities of thrift and enterprise and individual success that was most offended. All the values implicit in the philosophy of moral materialism seemed at stake.

The men and women who followed Theodore Roosevelt were not at all anxious to repudiate the profit system: they were merely angry and outraged with those who had made too good a thing out of the profit system. The American reverence for bigness was for the moment shaken. As one small businessman after the other was gobbled up, as the railroads squeezed the farmer, as it became shockingly clear that government of the people, for the people and by the people was turning into government of the corporations, for the corporations, and by the corporations—to borrow a phrase of the time—bigness, in the form of monopoly, took on the sinister shape of the figure of King Stork. Every trail of crookedness and corruption in government followed by the journalistic muckrakers, every smell that rose from the shame of the cities, led straight to the doorstep of Monopoly and Big Business: at the end of every path stood the figure of King Stork. It was the trusts that had poisoned the springs of economic well-being, that pulled the wires of invisible government, that had made a mockery of *laissez faire*. The aroused battalions of the middle class, alarmed as never before, moved forward to attack. In Theodore Roosevelt, whose mind fit its philosophy with a neatness that might have been tailored for the occasion, it found its natural leader.

III

In his agreement with Plutarch that the purpose of biography is to set up good examples, John Applegate would approve of Theodore Roosevelt's *Autobiography* with the same enthusiasm that he endorses the life-story of Andrew Carnegie. (It must be added, however, that he has never read this 647 page classic. His knowledge of Roosevelt the author comes from *African Game Trails*, which he received as a gift for subscribing to a magazine.) But unlike Carnegie's autobiography, with its mixture of naïveté and self-approval that gives us so many valuable insights into the character of the author, that of Roosevelt is curiously lacking in interest. The picture that comes through is that of a Public Figure who confesses nothing because he imagines he has nothing to confess

——not from self-congratulation, which is not one of Roosevelt's more noticeable traits, but rather from a conviction that he understands the motives that lie behind his every act: motives always admirable, always simple to the extreme. Beyond this there are pages and pages of energetic tedium, (Roosevelt did not write with a pen: he charged with it) enlivened by a notable collection of forceful platitudes. He is for marriage and exercise, against laziness and graft. He thinks that a man will succeed if he has "the right stuff" in him, will not if he has not. He does not care a rap for power, only for "the use that can be made of the substance." As long as a single copy of the *Autobiography* remains, it may judicially be said, Roosevelt's reputation as the apostle of the obvious is safe.

Nor do any of his other literary compositions manage substantially to shake this reputation. As good a sample of his serious thought as any (with the possible exception of his life of Oliver Cromwell whom he admired almost as excessively as did Carlyle) are the several essays brought together under the title *History As Literature.* There is a range of intellectual curiosity that commands respect, the stamp of an alert intelligence whose gravest fault lies in its inability to understand that there are certain walls that cannot be breached by mere derringdo, and a literary knowledge some of his critics might envy. The lecture delivered at Oxford in 1910 on *Biological Analogies In History* shows more than a superficial acquaintance with science, *The Search For Truth* reveals an ability to appreciate the ideas of such diverse philosophers as Henri Bergson and William James, and, if in the address delivered at the University of Berlin on *The World Movement* the tendency to think in terms of platitude is more marked, some of his observations, such as "Under modern circumstances the books we read, the news sent by telegraph to our newspapers, the strangers we meet, all tend to bring us into touch with other peoples," were destined to be repeated by other voices to larger audiences during the century.

It is in his lecture on *Citizenship In a Republic*, however, delivered at the Sorbonne during the barnstorming tour of 1910, that his claim to the title of apostle of the obvious is most boldly staked; and where, with the brevity imposed by the lecture form, he gives us the essence of his political thought. There is a great appearance of struggle, of mortal intellectual combat, but we soon come to see that most of this noise and display of battle is merely Theodore Roosevelt wrestling with himself——or, more exactly, with his extreme reluctance to come actually to grips with the problem that lies before him.

That Roosevelt was aware of the true nature of the problem is obvious. He knew as well as any man of his generation that the Industrial Revolution had more clearly defined class differences in America, that the movement of society was becoming less fluid, that the chief threat to the democratic idea ——this being before the rise of a new and unsuspected threat to democracy in the form of the corporate state——was contained in Marx's philosophy and program of class revolution. Such knowledge, implied by Roosevelt's complaint that the muckraking journalists (whom he christened) were building up revolutionary sentiment, was at the Sorbonne openly confessed.

"There have been," he said, "many republics in the past, both in what we call antiquity and in what we call the Middle Ages. They fell and the prime factor in their fall was the fact that the parties tended to divide along the line that separates wealth from poverty."

Well, if this was so, if this was the lesson of history, what was the answer? If here lay the threat to democracy, how was democracy to meet that threat? The question was an enormous one, and the fourth decade of the century would still find it lying unanswered, but plainly more was demanded than the crying out that such a state of affairs should not exist and the piling of one excellent sentiment upon another. Roosevelt, in these pages, suggests a man who, finding himself faced with a complicated problem in chess, his king in check, tries to improve his position by sweeping the pieces from the board. The most important thing he could find to say was:

> The gravest wrong upon his country is inflicted by that man, whatever his station, who seeks to make his countrymen divide primarily on the line that separates class from class, occupation from occupation, men of more wealth from men of less wealth, instead of remembering that the only safe standard is that which judges each man on his worth as a man, whether he be rich or poor, without regard to his profession or his occupation in life. Such is the only true democratic test, the only test that can with propriety be applied in a republic.

Who can possibly quarrel with this? Who can deny that "A good man is a brave man?" Or that "Character must show itself in a man's performance both of the duty he owes himself and the duty he owes the state?" But who, at the same time, can find in this anthology of homilies even an approach to the problem at hand, much less its answer? Roosevelt's reputation as a political thinker has admittedly never been high, but it is still uncomfortable to see him standing on the lecture platform of the Sorbonne and lending the weight of his own evidence to the remark Cecil Spring Rice made of him: "You must always remember that the President is about six."

To find fault with Roosevelt on this score, however, is to fall into the same kind of obviousness we would hold against him. "Full of platitudes," William Howard Taft decided finally, and Robert M. La Follette, in his autobiography, said: "Theodore Roosevelt is the ablest living interpreter of what I would call the superficial public sentiment of a given time, and he is spontaneous to his response to it." Yet it was exactly this spontaneous response to public sentiment, the way in which "the psychology of the mutt" found a reflection in his own, that enabled Roosevelt to become the outstanding leader of his time. Had his obviousness of thought not been brought to such a high point of development, were he less a master of saying exactly what the disgruntled citizenry wanted to hear said, he would probably not have become President. There is always John Applegate's division of human brows to be remembered, the highs on one side and the lows on the other, and the American reluctance to have one of the highs in the White House is notorious. Roosevelt, as emphatically as John Applegate, was against the highs.

"The closet philosopher," he said, "is of little use in actual governmental work."

IV

It would be a mistake, however, because of what one of Roosevelt's critics has called his unflagging approval of the Ten Commandments, to imagine that he brought nothing but evasiveness and platitude to bear upon the problem caused by the impact of the Industrial Revolution upon a political philosophy and system of government that had its origins in an agrarian society. Behind Roosevelt's famous "balanced judgments," often so well-balanced that they hang exactly in mid-air, meaning nothing at all, there lies a definite, though no less balanced, answer to the question *Is democracy possible?* Yes, replied Roosevelt, but there must be reform.

Reform may itself be interpreted as a form of evasiveness, especially by those who are impatient with the democratic process, and it may even be seen as an offshoot of cowardice. Georges Sorel, the prophet of violence who was so deeply to influence Benito Mussolini and others, who found in the principle of violence the basis of a new ethic, was unsparing in his contempt of those whom he always italicized as *worthy progressives*. No recent denunciation of reform improves in any way upon the invective Sorel pours out in his *Reflections On Violence*. "The specious reasoning of these gentlemen——the pontiffs of 'social duty'——supposes that violence may diminish in proportion as the intellectuals unbend to the masses and make platitudes and grimaces in honour of the union of the classes . . . It is enough to make one despair of sociology! If they had any common sense, they would remain quiet instead of devoting themselves to 'social duty.' Etc., etc."

Evasive or not——and it would seem, as an answer, evasive only to those who might find a similar evasiveness in any color not black or white——Theodore Roosevelt found his answer, or had the answer found for him by the progressives, in reform. He worked no miracles with reform, and his period as President was perhaps less productive of important social legislation than that of his successor William Howard Taft, but his answer, in broad outline, was identical with that later to be given by Woodrow Wilson and, later still, Franklin D. Roosevelt.

He had, it may be said, a clearer idea of his hopes, as expressed in a letter wherein he said that the idea toward which he was striving was to bring about a diffusion of wealth so as to avoid "the extremes of swollen fortune and grinding poverty," than of how to translate such hopes into reality. ("I cannot say," he confessed, "that I entered the Presidency with any deliberately planned and far-reaching scheme of social betterment.") He remains, however the first President of the United States openly to propose that the political authority of the state be used to discipline economics and bring about a wider distribution of wealth——a doctrine that would lie at the heart of Franklin D. Roosevelt's New Deal and find its most violent preachment in the hillbilly text of Huey P. Long.

One of Roosevelt's most explicit statements on political

theory, far worthier of him than anything said at the Sorbonne, is to be found in an article, *The Trusts, the People, and the Square Deal,* which is included as an appendix to his autobiography. But even here, it is interesting to notice, there is still a certain reluctance to take a clear and forthright stand. Instead of speaking in his own right, Roosevelt quotes from a speech made by Senator Cushman K. Davis in 1886, (Davis being of that earlier progressive school whose best representative was Henry J. Altgeld of Illinois, and whose thought was perhaps best summed up by Simon Patten in *The Premises of Political Economy*) and then adds his own approval—not, however, without introducing a few "balanced judgments" later on. But, in any case, the argument is stated:

> When Senator Davis spoke, few men of great power had the sympathy and vision necessary to perceive . . . that it was absolutely impossible to go back to an outworn social status, and that we must abandon definitely the *laissez-faire* theory of political economy, and fearlessly champion a system of increased Governmental control, paying no heed to the cries of the worthy people who denounce this as Socialistic.

This is still the central paragraph of progressive thought; the argument remains relatively unchanged. It has been recast more times than can be counted, as in Franklin D. Roosevelt's dictum that the United States could not go back to "horse-and-buggy days," but nowhere has it been greatly improved upon. Here the main battleground of American politics for the next four decades was staked off. The interminable arguments for and against Woodrow Wilson's New Freedom, for and against Franklin D. Roosevelt's New Deal, all the endless shouting and tumult, would be merely paraphrases and modifications of the arguments for and against Theodore Roosevelt's Square Deal. "The Sage of Oyster Bay" was of no great intellectual stature, the word sage having here a certain malicious content, but his shadow, which was the accumulated shadow of all the progressives he came to represent, was to linger across the American landscape when all that remained of his memory was the legend of his personality and tales of the strenuous life.

v

Enough has been written of Roosevelt's addiction to the strenuous life to make any further examination unnecessary ——Gamaliel Bradford, one of the gentlest of scholars, confessed that merely to think about all that energy made him feel tired. Even when Roosevelt sat in a rocking-chair he went on with his fury of living and, as John Burroughs recalled, should it happen that a mosquito needed killing, there was enough force expended to stun a bull elephant.

But what lay behind all that immense vitality, that furious celebration of muscular activity, that emphasis upon action that was to be his battlecry for fifty years? ("Get action. Don't fritter away your time. Create, act, take a place wherever you are and be somebody. Get action.") Why was he so contemptuous of the weakling, the timid, the uncertain? Such reasons as Roosevelt gives us are not altogether convincing. He believed he was the most honest man in the world, and the most sincere, yet in the end we come to feel he was always duping himself——or, if not that, trying to convince some disbelieving part of his mind of things he suspected were untrue. There is a gap somewhere, a missing center, the lack of a solid conviction whose absence must always be covered up by words. The portrait that emerges from Roosevelt's various hymns to the strenuous life, containing enough of a love of force to be a foreshadowing of the worship of force that was to become one of the most abnormal fixations of the century he helped inaugurate, is that of a man playing a part—a man of aggressive vanity and obdurate will, an ego-centered personality with a strong inclination toward self-dramatization.

Vanity, generally regarded as a negative quality, is one of the most positive human traits, probably having its roots in nothing more noxious than the normal desire to win the approval of others. (Self-love or narcissism, which is most often taken to be the meaning of vanity, is merely one of its offshoots.) A variable, taking different forms in different men, vanity may range from the self-abnegation of the anchorite, who expresses it by asserting the superiority of his spirit over the temptations of the flesh, to the more energetic ego of those who are determined to leave an indelible impress upon the tracks of time.

It is this latter form of vanity that we come across most frequently in politics. An art only by special definition, a science by no definition at all, politics is yet one of the more important forms of self-expression——one that men frequently turn to when other forms have proved inadequate or unsatisfactory. It is illuminating, even if obvious, that all the outstanding leaders of the Twentieth Century thus far——Theodore Roosevelt, Woodrow Wilson, Lenin, Mussolini, Hitler, Stalin, Churchill, Franklin D. Roosevelt——also had, or have, talents and ambitions in other fields.

Theodore Roosevelt was not ungifted as a writer and had he been more determined in this direction, and perhaps more rebellious against the standards and values of his class, it might not have been impossible for him to find a career in literature rather than politics, and to have become more reconciled to the frail body that made him unhappy as a youth. It was the determination to make over his body into a more adequate instrument, as everyone knows, that led him to embrace the strenuous life. But this determination, the ambition of a sickly boy born into a leisured class that has always emphasized sports in the manner of the English nobility, was clearly rooted in a sense of inferiority too galling for either will or vanity to stand.

One of the most revealing passages of Roosevelt's autobiography is that in which he tells how two boys made life miserable for him on a trip West, and how when he tried to fight them he was made to suffer the further humiliation of being handled with easy contempt. It was then, he tells us, that he made up his mind never again to be put into such a helpless position; when, having become "bitterly conscious that I did not have the natural prowess to hold my own, I decided to supply its place by training." Up to this point he is completely convincing: he wins our agreement as well as our sympathy. There then follows, however, a long paean to muscularity that is a cross between the chatter of a hunt breakfast and the noisier passages of Jack London——a younger contemporary with whom Roosevelt had much in common.

Roosevelt takes himself seriously here, just as he does in all his panegyrics to the strenuous life, but it is hard for us to do so. The picture is too forced, too desperate, too much the anxiety of a man who is fearful of dropping his pretense lest the whole thing tumble before his eyes. Roosevelt the he-man, dressed up as a hunter, seems always stalking the memory of the boy Roosevelt with the frail body: the image of inferiority must be destroyed again and again. There was other, more tangible game——lions, tigers, moose, grizzlies——but even in these exploits Roosevelt lacks conviction. The hunter's emotion is a hard one to communicate—as hard, perhaps, as the emotion of love—and it is probably unreasonable to expect of Roosevelt anything more than the surface record he gives us in *African Game Trails*. The question does arise, however, if he went hunting because he liked to hunt, or whether hunting was part of the game, the very complicated and elaborate game, he called the strenuous life.

"Playing a game"—time after time, in his books and correspondence, the phrase repeats itself: always we come across ideas linked to it. "The great game in which we are all engaged," he says in his autobiography, trying to get hold of the meaning of life: "It will be awful if we miss the fun," he remarked when the Spanish-American War broke out: "Get into the game," he advised the Boy Scouts. "Hit the line hard. Play the game for all you're worth."

What we have here, patently, is the most obvious kind of teen-age symbolism. But other than that, because of the persistence of the "playing a game" image and the ideas linked to it, there is the clear suggestion that Roosevelt actually did think of life as a kind of large performance. Crowded though his mind's eye was with his own image, there appears to have been scarcely a moment when he was not acutely conscious of the impression he was making on others.

"How I wish I *wasn't* a reformer, Oh, Senator!" he wrote to Chauncey Depew when he was Governor of New York. "But I suppose I must live up to my part, like the Negro minstrel who blacked himself all over."

Living up to his part as a reformer, he showed an equal brilliance in other roles. The Rough Rider could turn quickly into a naturalist: the big game hunter could shed his soiled garments and put on the academic weeds of a professor of history: the passionate advocate of muscularity could take his ease and discourse on art and *belle lettres*. And all the kaleidoscopic changes were made without apparent effort: each part was played with enough authority to convince the paying customers. "No other President of the United States," one admirer sums up, "ever put on such a corking good show."

With this it is easy to agree. The first American representative of Twentieth Century personalism in government, the first President of the United States openly to propose a more equitable distribution of wealth, Roosevelt was also the first exponent of Twentieth Century Barnumism in American politics. His understanding and appreciation of showmanship was almost as marked as that of the Great Educator. To his histrionic inclinations——the childlike love of dressing up in fancy clothes, the delight in presenting himself to admiring throngs, the joy of hearing his own words——he grafted a talent for press-agentry that enabled him to stamp his initials like a rancher's brand on the maverick hide of his time.

Under the influence of the four great founding fathers of modern journalism, Pulitzer and Hearst, Scripps and Bennett, (all of whom had profited by the lessons of Barnum) the press had taken on a new and powerful importance as the prime instrument of mass education, a position later to be challenged only by the motion-picture and radio, and Roosevelt was not long in discovering the truth of the newspaper-man's maxim that the only politician who does not need publicity is a dead politician. Reporters were never left without copy. If there was no news, Roosevelt "made" news ——preaching the gospel of simplified spelling, inviting Booker T. Washington to lunch, delivering himself of opinions on birth-control, divorce, the "full baby-carriage," the diet of blackbirds and the private life of Maxim Gorky. "The White House," he exclaimed, "is a bully pulpit!"

Having created a character, he knew how to live up to it ——when to put on his cowboy clothes, when to wear his Rough Rider suit; when to bellow, when to grin. The voyage of the American fleet around the world, the search for the River of Doubt in South America, the hunting trips in Africa ——he understood the publicity value of them all. More important than that, however, in a manner that would have compelled the admiration of the Great Educator, he knew how to exploit them so that his own name always managed to come first.

But his greatest performance, the role he played regularly for twenty years in all the corners of the globe, was that of the high priest of the strenuous life. The English knew of it, the Germans, the French and the Italians, the South Americans and the Japanese. Into it went all his imagination, all his aggressiveness, all his dramatic technique. He was always to look back on the day of his initial performance, when first he broke through the crust of relative obscurity and became the Hero of San Juan Hill, as the "greatest moment of my life." And that it was he, rather than Admiral George Dewey, who finally emerged as the first hero of the Spanish-American War is as much a tribute to his genius as a showman as to his personal bravery.

The Presidency, in 1900, seemed ready to drop into Admiral Dewey's lap. "There has been no hero so popular, no idol so worshiped, since General Grant received the surrender of Lee's army at Appomattox," editorialized *The Nation* of him. Within a short time after his return to America, however, thanks to his incredible self-contentment and political stupidity, the green shoots of his career withered and died under a hot blaze of criticism and satirical jeers.

The younger Roosevelt, stumping New York state as a candidate for Governor, was considerably wiser. His military reputation had preceded him. The whole nation knew how he led the attack at Kettle Hill (which he handsomely christened the "San Juan Charge") and how, under a hail of bullets, he sat on his mount with a blue polka-dot handkerchief flying from his sombrero, crying to his men:

"Are you afraid to stand up when I am on horseback?"

It was on Kettle Hill that the strenuous life was given its first public performance and, as a candidate for Governor, Roosevelt apparently thought it well to recreate as much of the original atmosphere as possible. He wore the same sombrero, the same clothes, the same bandana. On his special train were seven Rough Riders in uniform, and before each speech a bugler appeared on the rear platform to sound the cavalry charge. Not until then did the hero appear.

"You have heard the trumpet that sounded to bring you here," he began, after the cheering was over. "I have heard it tear the tropic dawn when it summoned us to fight at Santiago."

There would be other demonstrations of Barnumism in politics, both at home and abroad, more elaborate, more contrived, but here the method was discovered, here the technique described in full. The voice of the trumpet that tore the dawn at Santiago would go drifting along the years, repeated by other trumpets that heralded the appearance of more synthetic heroes in Berlin and in Rome, and, at home, echoed by the less glamorous but more native music of a hill-billy band, ridden by raucous voices offering to pass the biscuits and share the wealth.

And if Roosevelt's endless proselyting of the strenuous life, the celebration of energy born of the conflict between an originally weakling body and the aggressive impetus of a swollen will, would eventually cause Georges Sorel and others to call attention to the likeness between his ideas and those of Nietzche, and see him as representative of the imperial conqueror, the man on horseback, here again he was but a foreshadowing of the shape of things to come—again he might say, as he said during the campaign of 1912, "After all, was I not a great sounding board?"

In the end, however, for all of this, he comes to seem more like a figure out of fiction than of history—the last hero of the Age of Innocence, a frail boy with thick glasses who wanted to be big and strong and found, in America, the symbol of all he hoped to be. He ended by confusing America with himself, reading into the one the ambitions of the other, but while he never stopped celebrating himself, it is clear that he was also offering up a celebration of America ——a country brave and mighty, the opposite of all the sloth and indifference and cynicism he came to abhor, unique and splendid among the nations of the world. Perhaps he misread its character, even as he misread his own, but he never misread the measure of his own devotion. The flow of his invocation often falls into a jingo chant, and in his dreams were visions of golden islands to be invested beyond the seas, but even his imperialism has a certain rhetorical quality: it too was part of the strenuous life. Finding his symbol in America, and America in Theodore Roosevelt, he came to regard himself as its only authentic spokesman——there are times, indeed, when America seems to be the frail nearsighted boy who wanted to be big and strong, and Roosevelt the American dream. He thought of himself in epic terms, and his life in epic proportions, but both the terms and the proportions were those of a boy. His greatest misfortune, like all the heroes of the Age of Innocence, the Horatio Alger protagonists whom in so many ways he closely resembled, was that he never quite grew up. He was the Great Boy among the presidents, ego-driven and wilful, and it was perhaps inevitable that he should come to be remembered as the Boy Scout of the White House——peering through his thick glasses at all the great ambitions that were ultimately to elude his grasp and blazing, almost unconsciously, trails that others were to follow.

When he called himself a great sounding board, he reached an evaluation that can hardly be improved upon. We can only add that he was a greater sounding board than he knew. For while his legacy to the American inheritance consists of little more than a few phrases and the legend of his personality, the lines of his life are like isobars and isotherms that trace much of the American weather to come. There would be more striking evidences of personalism in government, more lavish exhibitions of political Barnumism, a more emphatic effort in the progressive direction. In each instance, however, it was he who broke the ground and showed the way. And as the century neared its halfway mark, and the various questions he raised still awaited their answers, he would come to take on a larger stature than the one he actually possessed—standing like a portent on the threshold of a new and different world, casting his shadow before.

·9·

HUEY P. LONG: KINGFISH
The American As Demagogue

DURING the years when Huey Pierce Long of Louisiana was making his bid for power, presiding over the political arena of his state in a way that reminded many people of Nero lording it over a Roman circus, John Applegate looked upon him with a certain amount of amusement. He liked to tell the customers who came into his drugstore that they, at any rate, knew better than to elect such a man to the United States Senate, and then, since some explanation for Long's career seemed necessary, put it down to the strange habit Southerners seemed to have of raising all sorts of queer people to high office——a sectional failing, interesting but disconcerting, like their fondness for cock-fighting and casual flirtation.

Much as he pretended to be scornful of Long, however, John Applegate never failed to read about him in the newspapers or missed a chance to listen to him over the radio. There was a time, moreover, during the depths of the Great Depression, when he even considered joining one of Long's "Share Our Wealth" Clubs——a loosely-knit fraternity which cost nothing to join ("To keep it a poor man's movement," Long explained) and whose members numbered, according to the expansiveness of the founder's mood, anywhere from five to nine million souls.

Now, while John Applegate may be regarded as a political innocent, he is nobody's fool. He knew, just as did all the

179

millions of persons who were part of the Share Our Wealth movement, that Long, who hoped and fully expected to be president, proposed to jettison the democratic framework and establish a system which, no matter what its surface disguise, would be a totalitarian state not altogether unlike the corporate state Mussolini had built up in Italy. For whatever his other failings, Long was never dishonest as to his ideas and theories of government—though, in strict accuracy, to call them ideas and theories credits them with a greater intellectual content than they actually had.

Most of the explanations so far attempted of Long's career fall into the category of explanation by epithet. He has been called a clown, a paranoiac, a superman, a fascist. Harnett Kane's documentary account of his rise and fall, *Louisiana Hayride*, reveals him as an unscrupulous demagogue with no larger equipment than a mania for power, and in the fiction he may be said to have indirectly inspired, such as John Dos Passos's *Number One* and Hamilton Basso's *Sun In Capricorn*, there is the same explanation in terms of demagogery and inflamed ambition. Both were present, and to a high degree, but the phenomenon of the Kingfish, as he liked to style himself, involved much more than that.

Long has been most frequently described as a product of the depression: a forceful rabble-rouser who captured the imaginations of millions of persons bewildered and desperate after years of bewilderment and misery. But this may be said, with equal truth, of a number of other persons who found a brief prominence during the depression years. The explanation is too convenient to be adequate. Long was the product of many different forces, and various tendencies converged in him, but his career largely depended, not so much upon the crash of 1929, which marked the end of one era, as upon Grant's hammering in Virginia and Sherman's march through Georgia, which brought about the downfall of another. The dialectic of John Calhoun sent forth great armies to do his bidding, and out of their defeat, and the ashes of the old plantation South, came a new and different society. One of the products of that society, perhaps an inevitable product, was Huey Long.

To compare John Calhoun and Huey Long is to make comparison more ridiculous than it generally is: even their names, standing together, manage to look absurd. Yet even as Calhoun proposed to alter the framework of democracy, denying its basic principles and speaking in terms that foreshadowed the creation of modern feudalism, so was Long to propose a complete jettisoning of the democratic system and bring to the language of totalitarianism, hitherto foreign in its accent, a rhythm and emphasis unmistakably American. The myth that holds Abraham Lincoln to have been an illegitimate son of John Calhoun takes on a greater creditibility when applied to Huey Long. The gaunt spokesman of plantation aristocracy would have detested the uncouth hill-billy from Winn parish, but, if he held to his logic, he could not have denied him as one of his offspring.

The pattern of society in the South before the Civil War is most conveniently thought of as a pyramid. The foundation of the structure, upon which its security and permanence depended, was the dark base of the slaves. At its apex, representing only a small fraction of the population, were the aristocrats, the landed overlords whose sons and daughters imparted to ante-bellum society those romantic and feudal characteristics which lend the popular conception of the old plantation its ideal coloring. Between the masters and the slaves, composing the bulk of the white citizenry, was the middle class ——the forgotten men and women of the Old South.

This class, containing roughly all those persons who did not fall within the aristocratic category, was composed principally of small farmers who, because of the economic caste system, had been driven to those parts of the various Southern States where the land was too poor to be cultivated by the plantation owners. Out of touch with even provincial centers of civilization, isolated in the hollows and the hills, they led lives of varying degrees of hardship. They were ignorant and superstitious. Their houses, not infrequently, were mud-plastered shacks that served as both home and stable. Pellagra, hookworm, and malaria were common diseases. Their women were broken at thirty and, to the horror of more than one traveler, their children often ate clay. They had little or no voice in the affairs of government. To hold office, because of the property requirements prevailing in many sections, was practically impossible. Admittance to the professions was equally difficult. They could not, because of the slaves and the odium attached to manual work, even hire themselves out as laborers without losing such caste as they had.

Nor were those a little higher in the social and economic scale much better off. Poverty, illiteracy, and a curious resentment toward learning were widespread—a resentment that makes the New England emphasis upon education, one of the happier by-products of Puritanism, the more striking by contrast. Sidney Andrews, a Bostonian traveling through the South in the late '50's, wrote in his notebook:

In the important town of Charlotte, North Carolina, I found a white man who owned the comfortable house in which he lived, who had a wife and three children, and yet had never taken a newspaper in his life. He thought they were handy for wrapping purposes, but he couldn't see why anybody wanted to bother with the reading of them. He knew some folks spent money for them, but he also knew "a-many" a house where none had even been seen. I also met several persons——whites, and not of the clay-eater class either——who had never been inside a

schoolhouse and who didn't mean to 'low their children
to go inside one . . .

In the upper part of South Carolina I stopped one night
at the house of a moderately well-to-do farmer who had
never owned any book but a Testament, and that was
given to him. When I expressed some surprise at this fact,
he assured me that he was as well off as some other people
thereabouts . . .

Between Augusta and Milledgeville, I rode in a stage-
coach in which were two of the delegates of the Georgia
Convention. When I said that I hoped the day would
soon come in which schoolhouses would be as numerous
in Georgia as in Massachusetts, one of them answered,
"Well, I hope it'll never come; popular education is all a
damn humbug, in my opinion"; whereupon the other re-
sponded, "That's my opinion too."

Andrews, obviously something of an intellectual snob and
not overly gifted with tact, was a fairly accurate reporter. His
observations are all substantiated by the accounts of many
other travelers, each of whom returned to his own people
with a feeling of amazement at the ignorance of poor white
Southerners and a consoling sense of superiority. It was these
same poor white Southerners, however, men who did not read
newspapers and were indifferent to education, who made up
the great bulk of the armies of the Confederacy, including
the Army of Virginia.

The letters they sent back home are letters such as men send
home from every war. As one reads them, however, the hand-
writing labored and the words misspelled, it sometimes seems
that in fighting the battles of the plantation *élite*, those who
wrote them were fighting against their own advancement.
The Civil War, as has been many times observed, did not altogether free the Negro. But it did free the Southern middle
class.

II

What happened in the South after the Civil War, the disintegration of a society, is best indicated by a simple statement of figures. In 1860, in the state of Georgia, there were twenty-one thousand registered land-owners. Ten years later, in 1870, the number of property holders had increased to fifty-three thousand, and the size of the average farm had fallen from 488 to 223 acres. What happened in Georgia happened in all the other Southern States. The large plantations, unable to be operated because of the breakdown of the plantation economy and the disorganized labor situation, soon fell to pieces. The hill-farmers acquired larger and more fertile tracts of land. Not dependent upon slave labor, used to a grilling routine of hard work, they were able to operate their newly acquired holdings at a profit. The war was followed, because of the breakdown of the plantation economy and a consequent reduction of acreage, by a substantial rise in cotton prices. This rise continued for several years. The newly liberated middle class began to reach out, cautiously at first, then more boldly, for some of the advantages and privileges formerly reserved for the plantation elect.

A new mercantile class also came into being. Formerly, on the all-sufficient plantations, the commissary had been the source of distribution for all the food, clothing and other supplies needed by the community. There were shops and markets in the cities, but in the rural districts, at some dusty cross-roads, a general store provided for most of the wants of the neighborhood. After the war, however, thousands of persons went into shopkeeping, the classic occupation of the middle class. "I found Georgia full of runners from the North," wrote one traveler in 1866. "They represented all branches of trade and generally reported that they were getting many orders . . . Everybody seems to have a passion for keeping store and hundreds of men are going into trade who should go into agriculture."

In the face of such change, all resulting from the collapse of the social system John Calhoun thought could be made imperishable, the representatives of plantation aristocracy began to retreat from life. Some of them, such as Wade Hampton and Senator Ben Hill, attempted to follow the pattern of the old order, but even they were eventually forced to surrender. "I would not care," wrote Admiral Raphael Semmes in 1869, "if I never saw a human being again." And General P. G. T. Beauregard, out of work and growing old, said in a letter to his son, "I feel like an old pea that has been left to dry in its pod."

Slowly, year by year, the social and economic pattern of the South was rearranged. By 1880 the rearrangement was complete. The middle class, consolidating its gains, had firmly established its position. There was no immediate displacement, however, of the old aristocratic leadership. The devotion of the former soldiers of the Confederacy to those who led them in battle, along with the fear that a division among the whites might involve a return to Carpetbag rule, was sufficient to keep them loyal, at least for a time, to their traditional leaders. But as they continued to grow in importance as a class, as group and individual ambitions grew larger, the fast diminishing leadership of the aristocrats began to be challenged. Then, toward the latter part of the century, after several years of depression, the Southern middle class, inarticulate so long, found its voice. It was the voice, roaring and blasphemous, of Benjamin Ryan Tillman——later to be known, after he declared his intention of running a pitchfork into "that old bag of fat, President Cleveland," as Pitchfork Ben, the Plowboy from Edgefield.

Even yet in Edgefield County, South Carolina, the Tillmans are remembered as violent men. They have become, with time's passage, almost fabulous for their physical strength and quickness with a gun. Ben was one of four sons. Two of his brothers were killed in shooting scrapes and a third, a lawyer named George, had to flee the country after he put an end to argument and settled a gambling dispute with a bullet. He managed to escape to Nicaragua where he joined the famous Walker filibustering expedition, but finally was captured and sent back to Edgefield where he served a term in prison.

Ben, then a gangling boy in his early teens, regularly went to the county jail to visit his brother; often he spent the night in his cell. George, who had spent two years at Harvard, was fond of reading and had seen the world. Often, so the fables say, he would read to his younger brother, booming out the words of Jonson, Scott, Shakespeare and Milton. "Whatever learning I have," Ben was later to declare, "I got from my brother George." And those evenings in the county jail, those candlelit sessions with the classics in the fecund silence of the South Carolina night, help explain the Elizabethan strain that runs through much of Tillman's oratory; as when he shouted, addressing an aristocratic gathering in Charleston: "You are the most arrant set of cowards that ever drew the fresh air of heaven."

The Tillmans, despite their long American history, belonged definitely to the middle class. They were innkeepers, operating a hostelry that drew its trade from the travelers going from Augusta, Georgia, to Columbia, the capital of South Carolina. Ben, the youngest son of the family, was born in 1847. He grew to manhood in Edgefield, not far from the Long Cane country where John Calhoun was born, spending the larger part of his time, as did most of the young men of the section, hunting and fishing and riding his horse. At the age of seventeen he suffered an injury to his eye which developed into an abscess of the socket. The infection spread and the youth, running a high fever, was expected to die. A Confederate army officer, however, stopping at the Tillman inn on his way to the front, removed the eyeball and lanced the abscess. Ben's life was saved but it took him two years to recover from the operation.

After the war, in which he did not see service, Tillman moved to a four-hundred-acre farm purchased by his mother when she sold the inn. From that time until 1886 he lived the uneventful life of a Southern dirt farmer. In the beginning, carried along by the rise in cotton prices, he prospered. But then came the panic of 1873, one of the severest the country has ever known, and, in the wake of the panic, a period of depression, crop failures and drought. The farmers, sinking farther and farther into debt, their farms mortgaged and their savings swept away, began to grow sullen and rebellious against the still dominant aristocratic leadership of the state. Tillman, who had become interested in politics several years before, sensed their temper and in 1890 decided to run for Governor of South Carolina. The first stirrings of Populism were in the air, though the Populists would not form their People's Party until the Omaha convention of 1892, and Tillman would later come roughly to represent the Southern reflection of the movement. His first campaign, however, was based on a single issue: *Turn The Aristocrats Out.*

"Say, you men who own the soil," he cried, "how do you like this wet-nursing, this patronizing, this insufferable insolence? How do you like being ruled by imbeciles and Bourbons? The State is in the hands of drones and vagabonds, aristocrats and lawyers in the pay of high finance. This state of affairs leads straight to hell."

Politics in the South have always been taken like a mixture of gin and moonshine corn, but Tillman's first race for Governor was one of the bitterest and most acrimonious struggles the section had ever seen. The Charleston *News and Courier* called him "the leader of a people who carry pistols in their pockets, expectorate on the floor, have no toothbrushes, and comb their hair with their fingers." His enemies said he was an agricultural Moses and a slacker——a charge that always sent him into rages of howling fury. He poured out all the invective at his command, classical and colloquial. And the rebellious middle class, hearing him say all the things they wanted to say, finding a reflection of their psychology in his, flocked to his support. He was elected by an overwhelming majority.

In his inaugural address, Tillman called his election a revolution. "Democracy, the rule of the people, has won," he said. "It has achieved a victory unparalleled in importance, and those who watched the abject surrender of our statesmen to the power of corporate money and class interests——all such must sing out with joyful hearts."

After two terms as Governor, during which a few minor reforms were effected, including the limitation of hours of labor in cotton-mills to sixty-six hours a week, Tillman was sent to the United States Senate. It was during his senatorial campaign that he threatened the person of President Cleveland and gained the name by which he is popularly remembered. As a Senator, an office he retained until his death, he became almost unrecognizably docile. Sometimes he roared, as in his earlier days, but in time even the roaring ceased. There is the temptation to believe he was investigating his own psychology when, after a drink in the fashionable Columbia Club, he remarked sarcastically, "It's a monstrous nice place. No wonder the cornbread and bacon fellows like it."

He died in July, 1918. The time was again a time of war and the newspapers had little room for him. He was an old man, and his battles were all behind him, and he belonged to an almost forgotten time. He had a larger importance, however, than has ever been understood. A minor figure, a provincial, he nonetheless introduced a new type into American politics—the evangelical demagogue—and marked the beginning of a wave that has not yet passed its crest. On the top of that wave, the perfection of the type he brought into being, rode Huey Long.

III

If Huey Long's influence had not extended beyond the boundaries of Louisiana, and if he had not there established a quasi-dictatorial regime, he would have no more claim to our attention than a host of other minor American politicians. His importance to John Applegate lies in the bid he made for national power, of enormous boldness and daring, and, more specifically, in the nature of that bid. Merely to say that he was a demagogue is to say nothing more incisive than that he made use of certain methods and tactics that are as old as recorded political history. As Mosca points out in *The Ruling Class*, the technique used by those who wish to exploit the sympathy of the masses has always been the same. It consists of pointing out, with proper distortion, the selfishness, stupidity, and material enjoyments of the rich and powerful, coupled with a promise to satisfy that common and rough-hewn sense of justice which would like to see a fairly general and more equitable distribution of both pleasure and pain.

The statement that Huey Long was a demogogue, then, tells us nothing. What was the nature of his demagogery and what was he saying that had never been said in America before? These are the questions that contain the nature of his importance to John Applegate.

The program that Long most depended upon, as everyone knows, was his Share The Wealth plan. A jerry-built structure of constantly changing design, it nonetheless had a fairly well-drawn blueprint. It proposed, as a first step, to liquidate all fortunes of more than four million dollars. Those who possessed such fortunes would be required, not to sell their holdings, but to transfer ownership to the United States Treasury, thus returning to the national coffers, according to Long's arithmetic, some one hundred seventy billion dollars. The plan then proposed (with considerable vagueness as to how it would be accomplished) to give every family in the United States a home, an automobile, and a radio; representing an approximate value of five thousand dollars. To do this, Long held, it would be necessary to spend about one hundred billion dollars. Beyond this, the plan proposed a minimum wage intended to give each family a cash income of not less than twenty-five hundred dollars a year, the guarantee of a college education to every child in the country, and the pensioning of all citizens when they reached the age of sixty-five.

This, stripped to its essentials, was Long's Share Our Wealth Plan——his presidential platform. That it was full of holes, and that its planks would make a leaky ship of state, needs no further stressing. Nor does the fact that Long was an economic ignoramus, thinking of the nation's wealth as so many poker chips which were to be piled on the table and redistributed among the players. All this, however, for our purposes, is relatively unimportant. What has to be stressed is the simplicity of the plan, its sweeping disregard of all the enormous problems whose terms are too difficult and complicated for John Applegate to understand. To be a demagogue, according to Aristotle, is to be one who flatters the people as the sycophant flatters the tyrant. It is to speak in the language of emotion, appealing to passion and prejudice, and, in making that appeal, not to mistake the masses for a learned academy. Long's Share Our Wealth Plan may insult the professional economic intelligence. It did not, however, insult the intelligence of the ten million voters whose support, according to general political estimate, he could have depended upon had he run for the Presidency.

How many other voters he might have attracted will never be known: his assassination in 1935 put the question beyond the test. But this, too, is unimportant. The fact remains that, in supporting Long, these millions were responding to a new and entirely different appeal——never before in American history had they been so plainly asked to jettison the democratic system and consent to the erection of a totalitarian society in its place.

Long's Share Our Wealth plan, in itself, was not new to America. It contained a good measure of old-time Populism, and the need for bringing about a more adequate distribution of the national wealth had been forcefully stated by Theodore Roosevelt. But not even Roosevelt, with his gift of showmanship, had been able to simplify and dramatize it as did Long. He represents the high peak of Barnumism in American politics. Having conceived a program, he went out to "sell" it, to "dramatize its appeal," to give it a new package and label. It may even be suspected that he played the clown for publicity reasons, agreeing with the Great Educator, whose star pupil he was, that any kind of advertising, even when it calls you a humbug, is good advertising.

The essential facts of Long's life may be briefly stated. He was born in a four-room log house in an upstate Louisiana parish in 1893. He was a book peddler, soap salesman, furniture salesman, patent-medicine salesman, and a cooking-contest organizer for the manufacturer of a lard substitute. He studied for a time at the University of Oklahoma and Tulane, passing his bar examinations with high honors and becoming a lawyer at twenty-one. Elected four years later to the Louisiana Public Service Commission, he was defeated for governor in 1924 when he was caught between a Klan and a Catholic candidate. In 1928 he was elected Governor and, before the expiration of his term, named to the Senate in 1930.

When he took office there was a widespread anticipation

of an unusual and conventional regime, but such anticipations were in no way commensurate with reality. What Long did, in effect, was to walk into the Governor's office, put his feet on the desk, and spit tobacco juice on the walls. The office of Governor until that time had always been considered one of importance, to be accorded at least a show of outward respect, and the antics of the Kingfish (a title borrowed, despite all the fables undertaken to explain it, from a popular blackface radio program of the time) left the people of Louisiana stunned and aghast. Nor did Long give them time to recover. He applied shock after shock, adding confoundment to confusion, until they, like his political opponents, were reduced to a state of impotent rage and the rest of the country was laughing its head off.

There was not a tradition or a ceremony he did not violate. He conducted the affairs of state from a bed in his hotel room. He engaged in brawls and fist-fights. He had reporters thrown from his presence. He surrounded himself with armed bodyguards and turned the State National Guard into a private army of storm troopers. He created an international incident by receiving in a pair of green pajamas the Commander of a German battleship, and was showered with pajamas from admirers all over the country. He turned the state legislature into a subservient body obedient only to his will. He drove his opponents from office, using "ripper" legislation when necessary, and filled the vacancies with hand-picked servants.

Throughout his term of office, however, Long did not neglect his constituents. He caused a network of improved roads and bridges to be built, free textbooks and school buses were provided for children, utility rates were cut, the poll tax was abolished. Even his bitterest enemies had to admit that, despite his totalitarian methods, Long had materially helped the poor whites and Negroes in their struggle against ignorance and poverty—recalling the similar admission forced from the enemies of Mussolini during the earlier years of his regime when he was devoting himself to what was publicized as the internal improvement of Italy.

By the time Long entered the United States Senate in 1930, at the end of the first year of the Depression, he had attracted national attention. No sooner had he taken his seat than he began to work out his economic program for the country. "I had been in the United States Senate only a few days," he said, "when I began my effort to make the battle for a distribution of wealth among all the people." In just a few months, with almost superhuman energy, he was preaching his new and revolutionary gospel.

"A leader," he said, "gets up a program and then he goes out and explains it, patiently and more patiently, until the masses get it. He asks for a mandate, and they give it to him, and he goes ahead with his program in spite of hell and high water. He doesn't tolerate no opposition from the old-gang politicians, the legislatures, the courts, the corporations, or nobody."

The technique implied here, of course, is the familiar one described by Machiavelli——that of gaining power and then using it to destroy or nullify all possible opposition. That this was Long's intention is plain. It was his expectation, openly expressed, to remain as President for sixteen years. During this time, as he saw it, the power of Congress and the Supreme Court would be emasculated and all authority, civil and military, taken into his hands. He also predicted that both major political parties would disappear and that, in their place, would arise a new mass party with himself as leader.

There arises, automatically, the question as to how much Long borrowed from the authoritarian doctrine of Mussolini and Hitler——the former already entrenched in power when Long was coming to prominence, the latter still building up his National Socialist party that was not to gain control of

Germany until several years later. Here no positive answer is possible. Long was not without a certain intellectual curiosity, and had a wide though superficial knowledge of that part of the world's literature known as the classics, but that he was familiar with any of the writings of the two European dictators is highly improbable. He had no knowledge either of German or Italian, and neither Mussolini's *I Discorsi della Rivoluzione* or Hitler's *Mein Kampf* had yet been translated; beyond that, he had no real interest in any kind of speculative thought, except in relation to the law. The methods and practices of Mussolini and Hitler were certainly known to him, however, and it would seem to follow that if he was influenced by them, as he unquestionably was, it was by their example rather than by a knowledge of their philosophy.

What he was saying, of course, more indirectly and in different terms, was what these dictators were also saying—that democracy had had its day and that a highly centralized state, directed and controlled by an all-powerful leader, must supplant the American system in order to solve the problems of the modern industrial state. There was, however, an important and profound difference. Whereas Hitler and Mussolini were advocating a program whose European inferences were too alien for John Applegate to understand, Long was talking his own native tongue. His was the only dialectic ever to be forged out of Joe Miller's joke-book and Biblical misquotations. Those who listened needed no knowledge of Marx or Spengler. It was simply a matter of dividing the national wealth as the ancient Hebrews had divided land and cattle. The two books he left as part of his legacy, his autobiography, *Every Man A King*, and his posthumously published *My First Days In The White House*, a kind of Alice-in-Wonderland account of what would happen when he came to the Presidency, are almost pathetic in their crudity. But as the first body of modern American totalitarian thought derived entirely from native life and experience they have considerable value.

These two books, which were really intended as political pamphlets, first of all confirm the fact that revolutionary or demagogic appeals can be made to serve the purposes of the right as well as the left. The political argument put forward, in hill-billy terms, is essentially the same argument brought forth by Hitler in *Mein Kampf* and Mussolini in *I Discorsi della Rivoluzione*. Entrenched privilege and greed, standing in the way of the masses, must be destroyed. But while Hitler's bible is confused with twisted borrowings from Fichte, Hegel, Treitschke, Nietzsche and others, and Mussolini's inflamed hymn to Latinity full of echoes of Lenin, Pareto and Sorel, the gaunt life-story told by Long is as bleached of philosophical pretense as a skeleton's skull. All it contains, other than the story of his own life which is made to fit the familiar Horatio Alger pattern, is the collection of Joe Miller jests and Biblical distortions already mentioned, and a final promise to look after the material requirements of those willing to exchange political freedom for economic security—a swap, as much recent history has demonstrated, that men and women are sometimes willing to make.

The tragedy of Huey Long, for he was a tragic rather than a comic figure, was that it lay within his ability to be a great democrat. His feeling for the common people was as genuine as affected, and there can be no doubt of his enormous following. At first glance it may seem that he, too, was championing the people against the elect, as when in the Senate he defied the House of Morgan, but in reality, like all those of the authoritarian creed, he was proposing the creation of a new ruling *élite* composed of those who would center about him had his ambitions been fulfilled.

It is interesting to see how he tried to square his general

doctrine with that of the Declaration of Independence. In that passage of *My First Days In The White House* where he anticipates his inauguration as President, he writes, "I laid aside my prepared speech and closed my inaugural address with these words:

> I promise that children shall not come into this life burdened with debt, but on the contrary, shall inherit the right to life, liberty and such education and training as qualifies them and equips them to take their proper rank in the pursuance of the occupation and vocation wherein they are worth most to themselves and to this country.

Just as it is not enough to cry demagogue, so is it not enough to laugh aloud. For howsoever crude Long's thought may strike the intellectually sensitive, it did not seem crude to the depression-ridden millions who found in it a fair reflection of their most immediate hopes and dreams. In a period when all values had been corroded or swept aside, after the long derision of the 1920's characterized by a mindless cynicism that denied every value simply because it was a value, when everything that had happened in America was laughed at for no other reason than that it had happened, when the promise of American life seemed to have turned into the promise of the breadlines, it was inevitable that Huey Long should emerge as the most revolutionary leader of the masses. For what he did, in a time of want and misery, was no more than to strip the American philosophy of moral materialism of its last vestige of morality and preach the gospel of comfort which, in the last analysis, would seem to be what had come to be accepted as the American ideal. To want, and want, and want again——ever since the Civil War this had been the principal lesson of the American's education. The ideal reflected by the political slogans of each era——the full dinner pail, 'normalcy,' a chicken in every pot—was always the ideal of comfort. How American, then, how native in root and branch, was Long's program of sharing the wealth. A home, an automobile, a radio, twenty-five hundred dollars in cash each year——what more could the human animal desire?

It would be too much to expect of John Applegate, especially during the years of the Depression, to question the validity of this ideal——not only because he holds to it, and has been educated to believe in it, but also because the general misery of the Depression blocked his chance of understanding (relatively slight under the best of circumstances) that the ideal of comfort, in the end, offers no larger inspiration than Barnum's ideal of money-getting or the ideal of millionairedom. Man must have goods in order to live, and will go to extreme limits to get them, but if goods and comfort are all he wants, goods and comfort and nothing else, he can never have enough——as two cars in every garage are better than one, so are four better than two: it goes back to the old progression, "Pigs for more pigs for more pigs." Man, as an animal, knows animal hunger. But to say, as did Long, that this is his only hunger, is to ignore and deny those rational and spiritual attributes which are presumed to set him apart as a species from the other animals. It is to deny, ultimately, because of his animal hunger, that he is human at all.

This was the denial, which lies at the heart of all the totalitarian creeds, of Huey Long——a denial to which he added a specific warning. Out of all the words he uttered there was but one sentence of truly penetrating insight. "When the United States gets fascism," he said, "it will call it anti-fascism." It was a cynical remark, and the cynical were amused, but it was full of hidden meaning. For what he was saying, again as if he were a careful student of Machiavelli, was that even the most audacious despot must beware of shocking the sentiments, convictions or prejudices of a people, and that when and if fascism comes to America, it must find its expression in native American terms——such terms as he himself set out to forge.

There are Americans far more notable than the Kingfish from Louisiana. The historian of the future may probably find it unnecessary to give him more than a footnote——possibly dismissing him by saying he wanted to be dictator because he could not immediately be President. Few of John Applegate's countrymen, however, have given him more to remember.

FRANKLIN DELANO ROOSEVELT
The American and the Revolution

THE ESSAYIST, presuming to write of Franklin Delano Roosevelt at a time when he is still President of the United States, will do well not to fall into the mistake of confusing himself with posterity. He will remember that the path of any man's life is suggestive of the path of the electron, whose direction cannot yet be foretold in advance, and he will also remember the mordant Spanish proverb which holds that it is impossible to weigh the good or the evil that is in a man until he is safely dead. He will keep in mind, also, the fact that history is a thing in flux, shifting and uncertain, and that, as Machiavelli wrote, the present always seems less heroic than the past. He will, in short, render unto posterity that which concerns posterity and not take it upon himself to be a prophet.

There are, in addition, certain practical difficulties to overcome. The time is one of mass publicity, when the methods of P. T. Barnum are being applied throughout the world, and, as is always the case with a President, the various mechanisms of celebration and defamation are forever at work. A President is the leader of a political party. It is important to that party, which has an economic stake in the matter, that he be presented in the best possible light. It is no less important to the party of the opposition, which also has an economic stake in the matter, that he be made to appear inept and incompetent, if not a downright danger. Few men in public life have been criticized more harshly than George Washington. Jefferson, "The People's Friend" to those who followed him, was castigated by the Federalists as a wanton revolutionary who, among other things:

> retires to lash his slaves at home;
> Or woo, perhaps, some black Aspasia's charms,
> And dream of freedom in his bondmaid's arms.

So it has been in politics: so will it be always. Franklin Roosevelt's reputation as the "most hated" man ever to sit in the White House is merely another reminder that slander and calumny are the two most tireless handmaidens of politics, endlessly spinning, always at work. The very hatred Roosevelt has aroused, however, will be useful to the future historian as a gauge of his importance. Only the most innocuous among the Presidents, such as Calvin Coolidge, the latterday Puritan who presided over the Babylon of the Boom Age, give no offense. Posterity, if only because of the hatred he has called forth, will know Franklin Roosvelt as one of the foremost American Presidents. And the future student of history, thumbing the record of a troubled time, will also find evidence of a great warmth of affection——hatred alone does not elevate a man to the presidency for a series of successive terms.

John Applegate, who calls himself an independent Republican, voted for Roosevelt in 1932 and again in 1936. In 1940 he voted for Wendell Willkie, a man who came to rather simple discoveries fairly late in life, such as that the world is a relatively small place after all, but whose very innocence in the matter enabled him to preach them with winning energy and gusto. It was but a little more than a year after he cast this vote, however, when John Applegate began to feel thankful that he had been on the losing side. Certain values change with circumstance and the bombs that dropped on

Pearl Harbor on December 7, 1941, bringing home to the American for the first time "the lines of a new concentration" Henry Adams had so clearly discerned in the Spanish-American War, brought also an enormous change in values to John Applegate. From feeling a little disgruntled with President Roosevelt for having gotten into the White House for a third term, he began to feel, instead, that in a time of extreme crisis, he was the best man for the job. The confirmed opponents of President Roosevelt continued in their opposition, and their hatred was in no way diminished, but as far as John Applegate was concerned they were shouting down a well. It was as much a waste of time and energy as the attempt made to re-elect Herbert Hoover in 1932.

In that year, however, it cannot be said that John Applegate voted for Franklin Roosevelt: he voted, as has been repeatedly remarked, *against* Herbert Hoover. In an era of almost total negation, when for the first time in his history the American was without any real sense of purpose or direction, he cast a negative vote. And that it was Roosevelt for whom he voted, rather than some other Democrat, was due more to the workings of party politics, and the indefatigable energies of a party politician named James Farley, than to any pronounced demonstration of exceptional ability on the part of Franklin Roosevelt.

It is true that Roosevelt had been Assistant Secretary of the Navy in the cabinet of Woodrow Wilson, as well as the Democratic candidate for the vice-presidency in 1920, and had served two moderately distinguished terms as Governor of New York, but one has only to go to his public papers to understand that he came to the White House with ideas as hazy and uninformed as those of the first Roosevelt; the major part of his policy, during the earlier part of his first administration, consisting of nothing larger than the traditional American willingness to try anything once.

In his speech of acceptance, delivered before the Chicago convention, Roosevelt put forward his interpretation of recent American history and gave an outline of his policy. During the period of post-war expansion, he said, "there was little or no drop in the prices that the consumer had to pay although . . . the cost of production fell very greatly; corporate profit resulting from this period was enormous. At the same time little of that profit was devoted to the reduction of prices [and] the consumer was forgotten." Corporate surpluses, he continued, had gone "first, into new and unnecessary plants which now stand stark and idle; and secondly, into the call money of Wall Street, either directly by the corporations, or indirectly through the banks. Those are the facts. Why blink them?" In a time of crisis, he went on to say, the Republican administration had gone to the aid of the interests at the top of the pyramid to the neglect of the common folk at the bottom. "And there," he exclaimed, "we are today!"

Roosevelt then proceeded to outline his remedy for the situation. First and foremost, government must economize. The Prohibition amendment must be repealed, while the return of the open saloon prevented. A kind of pure-stock-and-bond act must be enacted in order to protect the investing public. A program of well-planned public works, as self-sustaining as possible, must help reopen the avenue to employment. Agriculture must be aided by an easing of credit, and a voluntary reduction of agricultural surpluses made part of the general objective. "Such a plan as that, my friends," said Roosevelt, "does not cost the Government any money, nor does it keep the Government in business or speculation."

The gulf that separates this program from the accumulation of trial and error, good and bad, wisdom and folly, known as the New Deal is wide indeed. The manner in which it came to be bridged must await a later and more detailed telling than this. It is clear, however, that Roosevelt and his associates in the Democratic party held to the same interpretation of American history as did the Republicans. Both parties accepted the prevailing instruments of owner-ship and production as permanent. Both pledged to take the government out of business. Both granted the profit motive to be the prime motor in setting and keeping real property in action to produce wealth, and that a fair distribution of wealth would be brought about by the automatic operation of the price and wage mechanism in the open market.

That both the Republicans and Democrats should have held this general view is not surprising. Even in 1932, despite the deepening of the Depression, most Americans took established folkways, mores, and sentiments for granted. And if both Republicans and Democrats betrayed a large ignorance of history, and a grave failure to understand that the time of domestic challenge to the American system had finally ar-rived, when, as James Madison had foreseen would happen, the great mass of people were without property of any kind, only those who have never been privileged to listen to the un-buttoned conversation of professional politicians expect them to be historically informed.

The question *Is democracy possible?* rarely loomed larger than in 1932, but neither political party seemed aware of its existence. It was almost as if the conditions that saw the for-mation of the American system still prevailed. There was, moreover, judging from their platforms, a general belief on the part of both parties that American history was closed. Even the implication of development was denied——the fact that history is a thing in flux and that its only certainty is the certainty of change. The problem seemed to be, in large part, how to take a society that had always been dynamic, whose equilibrium had been the equilibrium of the spinning top, and make that society static. Both parties, it now appears, looked to a time when the wheel of the future would return some era of the past. The particular era that was to be "recovered" and "restored," however, went unnamed——a matter, it would seem, of no particular consequence.

All this would be of minor interest did it not involve Franklin Roosevelt. Having already gone beyond the limits we originally defined, and anticipated that posterity will come to regard him as one of the foremost American presidents, the obligation of trying to determine the probable reasons for such a distinction cannot be avoided. We begin, then, with the fact that he came to the Presidency with ideas and theories totally different than those he would later espouse, that his whole campaign in 1932 was conducted on the basic principle of the professional politician, "Don't rock the boat," and that, called upon to head the American system at its moment of greatest domestic challenge, he seemed at best only dimly aware that such a challenge existed.

What, specifically, was this challenge? A volume larger than this might be written in answer, for the whole of American history is involved, but at least its essentials may be stated. Jefferson, whom we have preferred to regard as the chief philosopher of American democracy, held certain fundamental beliefs. Perhaps the most important of these, from which most of the others were derived, was that it would take the country from five hundred to two thousand years to become settled. The society he foresaw, in his *Notes On Virginia*, was an agrarian state in which each citizen would have a positive property stake, most generally in the form of a small plot of land.

Much has been made of the fact that Jefferson, in writing the Declaration of Independence, substituted "the pursuit of happiness" for the customary "property" of John Locke. It is foolish to deduce from this, however, that Jefferson did not place a high value on property as a social stabilizer, or that the word in itself has any sinister or undemocratic connotations. Locke himself, in his *Concerning Civil Government*, clearly states that by property he means "that property which men have in their persons as well as goods"——property, in other words, directly concerned with the pursuit of happiness.

Jefferson's theory was essentially a simple one; perhaps too simple for the indifferent world of fact. Democracy, he understood, cannot rely on good intentions alone: the individual citizen, through the possession of property, must look upon his welfare and that of the state as being mutually interdependent. The prime object of statecraft, in keeping with the theories of the French Physiocrats to whom Jefferson was greatly indebted and whose agrarian system seemed to fit American conditions perfectly, was to hold manufactures and commerce to an indispensable minimum. The doctrine that appears in Jefferson's writings again and again is that these and the professions are "sterile" occupations, deriving their sustenance from the "extractive" industries (principally farming) which are impoverished when the non-productive or "sterile" occupations are too greatly expanded.

Even Jefferson's belief in the people as the ultimate guardians of liberty rested on his agrarian view of the future. Fully aware of the dangers of a weak government, he feared the abuse of authority more. The best safeguard against such abuse, he concluded, was to place the control of government as directly as possible in the hands of the people. However dangerous this might be in Europe, where "in the hands of the *canaille* of the cities . . . it would be instantly perverted to the demolition and destruction of everything public and private," it could not help but prove highly beneficial in the democracy of farmers and villagers, all property owners, which he envisioned.

Yet even as he was putting forth these views in the *Notes*

On Virginia, forces were already at work that would transform the United States from an agrarian community to the largest industrial society the world had ever seen. The economic and political developments of the next century were to undo nearly all that had been accomplished by the Jeffersonian movement, and, again with the irony of history, prove the essential soundness of Alexander Hamilton's insight into the dynamics of the Industrial Revolution, along with the general correctness of his view of the future.

But our present concern is not with Jefferson, or Alexander Hamilton, but with Franklin Roosevelt. By 1932 the moment of challenge that Jefferson had feared, and Madison foreseen, had indisputably arrived——the nation was not a nation of independent property-holders, each with a stake in the economic order, but preponderantly a nation of the propertyless. How might their interest, and the interest of America, be made reciprocal? This was the challenge and the problem. What answer had Franklin Roosevelt?

To say that he was unaware of the challenge, and had no answer, is to strike a judgment that is better left to a later and more informed generation. We can only examine his addresses and papers of the time and report that nowhere does such an awareness come clearly through. The grave crisis into which the nation had fallen, it would seem, was due solely to a band of wilful men, "magnates of finance," who sought to avoid the dangers of competition and refused to hand out their rewards of profit to wage-earners and consumers. But this interpretation of history, correct though it was, indicates a knowledge of history that goes no further than the day before yesterday. Wall Street was put on trial when the American system was at stake. The guilt of monopoly capitalism was important, and the money-changers must indeed be driven from the temple, but the larger and more pressing issue was that with which the country had been faced since the turn of the century—— Can democracy meet and solve the problems of an industrial society?

To tax Roosevelt with not having discovered the answer to this question, however, is to tax him for not being the wisest man of his time. The issue lies still before us, in the path of every man to get around as best he can, and no final solution has been forthcoming. But Roosevelt's claim to greatness, it may be said, does not lie in his distinction as a political philosopher. He is no Jefferson, no John Taylor of Caroline, (undeservedly neglected, the best philosopher of Jeffersonian democracy) no Daniel Webster, no John Calhoun. The ambition of his thought, at least in general, rarely rises above the level of those hearth-to-hearth chats he sometimes broadcasts to John Applegate over the radio. His first inaugural address is as good a sample of his intellectual approach as any.

"Only a foolish optimist," he said, "can deny the dark realities of the moment . . . Plenty is at our doorstep, but a generous use of it languishes . . . Primarily this is because rulers of the exchange of mankind's goods have failed . . . Practices of the unscrupulous money-changers stand indicted in the court of public opinion . . . They know only the rules of a generation of self-seekers. They have no vision, and when there is no vision the people perish . . . Yes, the money-changers have fled from their high seats in the temple of our civilization . . . We may now restore that temple to its ancient truths . . . We do not distrust the future of essential democracy. The people of the United States have not failed. In their need they have registered that they want direct, vigorous action. They have asked for discipline and direction under leadership. They have made me the present instrument of their wishes. In the spirit of the gift I take it."

Is it merely what Machiavelli called "knowing the good together with many other things that are displeasing to us," that makes us see this as an exercise in rhetoric and little else? Is it quibbling to ask what "ancient truths" shall be restored to the temple; what is meant by "essential democracy?" Or is this address of Roosevelt, fairly representative of them all, merely the statement of an adroit and skillful politician who knows, even better than did his distant connection Theodore, how to say most eloquently those things John Applegate wants to hear said?

It may be a judgment of posterity, however, that while Roosevelt was not a political philosopher, he was a great leader. Of this there can be no question. Returning to our un-proved premise that nearly everything that happens in modern politics is eventually traceable to the passions and prejudices of men, and that there is a constant interplay of forces be-tween the leader and the led, it is clear that Roosevelt emerged as the great leader of the first half of the Twentieth Century in America because he was able to make articulate the passions and prejudices, the hopes and fears, of the great majority of his countrymen, particularly the dispossessed.

Indirect proof of this is given by the failure of the com-munists of the period who looked upon the Depression as the final agony of capitalism, paving the way for their triumph. It was true that the larger part of labor in the United States was unorganized and that most trade unionists wanted a larger share of the profits of capitalism rather than an overthrow of the capitalist system, but it was imagined that the "objective realities" of the Depression had profoundly altered the psy-chology of American wage-earners and prepared them for a break with the past. Such hopes, however, were not realized. Many causes may be assigned for the failure of the com-munists, but foremost among them was their almost religious conviction that New York was Moscow and the Middle West the steppes, which, together with a vocabulary and vision of history derived largely from the pages of Marx, made most of what they were saying totally incomprehensible to most

is that if George Washingto
tree, and say "Father, I cann
hatchet," he should have. A
somehow manages to believe

It is generally supposed th
but this does not have to be tl
up about Patrick Henry, fo
phrase, "Give me liberty or
calculable value in keeping J
racy vital and alive. The my
here the reality might better
his nearest approach to an
founding fathers, whom he l
men, has lent him a respect f
that respect, a certain regard

The writings of Georges S
(on the theory, it would app
have to teach are better not
calist philosopher who ended
ceived the positive value and
who are participating in a g
always picture their coming
cause is certain to triumph.
opinion, is dependent on myt
be taken as a whole, as an his
down into its separate eleme
he cites those that were const
by the Reformation, by the
followers of Mazzini.

Sorel, though it would n
live to see how his theory o
the purposes of Hitler and
myth of Latinity and the oth
But the wrong uses to which

Americans. Behind this failure, however, as the election returns of 1932 and 1936 made plain, there loomed the larger fact that the ethic or emotion of democracy still played an enormous part in the shaping of American psychology.

The nation lay like a great and stricken ship that had drifted into a stagnant sea, its motors idle and its pistons still, but only a handful of Americans, the intellectuals of the extreme left most notably among them, believed that the ship was doomed. Not even during the banking disaster of 1933, when one liberal weekly complained that Americans were too cheerful, did John Applegate believe that democracy had failed. Perhaps his critics are correct in their castigations of his optimism, seeing his belief that "everything will work out all right" as nothing more than the uninformed hope of a child, but such castigations fall short of their purpose in that they fail to consider that more than optimism is involved.

John Applegate is a human being. His education has been greatly neglected. The ideal that has been held up to him, more often than not, is the ideal of comfort. He believes in some vague thing called progress without once suspecting that progress may not necessarily mean improvement. Of the historical roots of democracy, and the moral and spiritual principles with which it is illumined, he knows but little. Those who expect too much of him are as likely to be as disappointed as those who expect nothing at all. Yet for all his failings, which no amount of evasion can hide or sentimentalism undo, he clings to his democratic faith.

What is this faith? It is, in one sense, all things to all men. Sometimes, as if the substitution of three words for one were an aid to clarification, it is said that democracy is a way of life. But what kind of way? In a nation of one hundred forty million people there are bound to be exactly one hundred forty million different ways of life. It would be folly to presume that over all these separate ways there bends a common demo-

cratic sky: or that or
have each examined th
Yet unless it be admit
not believe in democr
thropic denial of his
preponderant number
wide community of t
racy is based on a beli
end, for all the various
would seem to rest on
be defined as the Ame

Definitions, howev
meant, specifically, a
sibly relates some hist
to explain some practi
of myth in any cult
pologists. But what se
in the United States.
should know better tl
Washington and the
understand that the fo
in their own economi
dubious character w
Such knowledge on t
together admirable. It
more about such thin
and novelists tried to
and the dead, have f
jeered at nearly all th
respect. Such astring
though in their eman
satirists had a firmer
than what to respect
foolhardiness, preferr

danger, need not blind us to the fact that democracy has its myth as well——no less important, as an historical force, than the myth of the French Revolution, or the myth of Mother Russia that the Soviets found so valuable in their struggle against Nazi Germany.

The importance of the democratic myth as an historical force in the United States has found little modern appreciation. The chief reason for this would seem to be the "unscientific" nature of the myth in a time perhaps overly impressed with the methodology of science: the myth being, as Renan said of all human affairs, "an approximation lacking in precision and gravity." Political science, for instance, according to one of its practitioners: "heaves to the wind all of the old-time paraphernalia of democratic theory. For the many sophistries which have sprung from such abstractions as the idea of natural rights, the dogma of equality, or the doctrine of the general will, it does not even bother to apologize. It frankly agrees with the critics of democracy that the sole measure of truth for any political philosophy is its conformity with objectively established facts."

Such a view is fairly typical of the intellectual approach of a whole generation. The disavowal of the democratic myth during the derisive era that lay between the end of one World War and the beginning of another, was but part of a larger disavowal that managed to include all things American. This disavowal, however, is wrongly taken solely as a manifestation of "irresponsibility": a charge that comes with but little grace from some of those who make it. There was also involved a kind of inverted idealism——a genuine feeling of shame over the standards and values of Boom Age America,* and, in

---

* "By 1928," Malcolm Cowley quotes F. Scott Fitzgerald as saying, "Paris had grown suffocating. With each new shipment of Americans spewed up by the Boom the quality fell off, until toward the end there was something sinister about the crazy boatloads. They were no longer the simple pa and ma and son and daughter, infinitely superior in their qualities

relation to politics, an earnest effort to give a certain scientific precision to political thinking and, by virtue of that precision, a denser gravity. But the end result of this attack, whatever its conscious or unconscious motives, was to introduce the same moral skepticism that Proudhon in his *Justice in the Revolution and in the Church* saw as a social danger in France some seventy-five years before the Nazi storm-troopers took possession of Paris.

"France," wrote Proudhon, "has lost its morals. Not that, as a matter of fact, the men of our generation are worse than their fathers . . . When I say that France has lost its morals I mean that it has ceased to believe in the very principles of morality, a very different thing. She has no longer moral intelligence or conscience, she has almost lost the idea of morals itself; as a result of continual criticism we have come to this melancholy conclusion: that right and wrong, between which we formerly thought we were able to distinguish dogmatically, are now vague and indeterminate conventional terms; that all these words, Right, Duty, Morality, Virtue, etc., of which the pulpit and the school talk so much, serve to cover nothing but pure hypotheses, vain Utopias, and unprovable prejudices."

Proudhon might have been writing about the United States in the 1920's and 1930's instead of France in the Nineteenth Century. [Are not these "pure hypotheses, vain Utopias, and unprovable prejudices," for example, equivalent to the "old-time paraphernalia of democratic theory" which political science says must be cast to the winds?] The record of the time as written in its novels and biographies, criticism and drama, is largely the record of a wholesale onslaught against all conventional and established American values——the dominant tone is dislike, if not hatred, of the United States.

---

of kindness and curiosity to the corresponding class in Europe, but fantastic neanderthals who believed something, something vague, that you remembered from a very cheap novel."

The whole expatriate movement, perhaps the most interesting footnote to the Boom Age, was founded on little more than hatred if Malcolm Cowley, the historian of the movement, is correct in his exegesis. It may have been that the Boom Age expatriates were seekers after the good life, and like Henry James in another era were attempting to refute the ideals of commercialism by celebrating those of art, but such an interpretation would depend too much on charity to be convincing. "The expatriates," Cowley writes, "were pushed eastward by the need for *getting away* from something"; trying to escape "some quality of American civilization that they carried within themselves."

But during this era of derision and denial, what of John Applegate——who should by now appear, if our portraiture has been at all competent, as a fairly adequate representative of the society both the expatriates in the 1920's, and the communist fellow travelers in the 1930's, were trying to escape. To say that he invites all the arrows in the quiver of satire is to metaphrase the obvious: to say that he has been a convenient whipping-boy, a sort of secular St. Sebastian for the literati, is to say what Sinclair Lewis, the creator of George Babbitt, has found it necessary to admit at greater length.

John Applegate, it is true, has never heard of the expatriates: his innocent idea of a fellow traveler is the man who sits next to him on the day-coach. It would be wrong, however, because of this, to imagine he was unaffected by the sustained attack upon all the things in which he believed. One result of this indiscriminate onslaught has been described by Rebecca West in an essay which tells, in part, of a trip she made to the United States not long after the publication of *Babbitt*. Often she was a guest in the homes of businessmen and she writes that she cannot remember a single time when her host or hostess failed to make some remark, with a deprecating laugh, such as "I'm afraid you'll find us terrible

Babbitts," or, "Well, you know us already. Our name is Babbitt."

"The victim of satire," Miss West concludes, "being as uncertain as the satirist of what deserves to be attacked and what to be defended, could not hit back. He had therefore no other resort than to pass over to the satirist's side and join in the laughter."

What effect these two decades of derision, coupled with the Depression, had upon the American psychology can only be surmised. There can be no doubt, however, but that it was considerable. Yet with the election of Franklin Roosevelt in 1932, and more particularly his reëlection in 1936, it was plain that the American held to his belief in the democratic system. Challenged by the Marxian myth of catastrophic revolution, and the myth of native dictatorship that was forming about Huey Long, the American myth, though shaken, managed to endure. Democracy might be a joke, and the United States the waste-land, but, if so, John Applegate wanted to abide in the desert and laugh.

The election of Roosevelt in 1932 can now be seen as marking the beginning of the end of the era of denial that began after the War of 1914-18. With his coming to the Presidency the search for new values and meaning in American democracy was slowly to begin again. And Roosevelt, in many ways, was the leader of the search, pointing its objective and general direction. His greatness as a leader depends not upon his rhetorial ability to sway the multitudes (by which definition Hitler would be equally great) but upon his articulation of those essential principles that lie at the heart of the democratic faith. In a time when the democratic system stood at bay, when by the pragmatist's rule only the totalitarian societies appeared "to work," he emerged as one of the great champions of democracy. History may conclude otherwise, for it is hugely indifferent to judgments made in advance, but it would seem that for this alone his place in the gallery of great Americans will be splendid and secure.

II

Shakespeare gets some of his best effects, as Maurice Baring has noted, by using the simplest words, sometimes by sheer exclamations like "O! o! o! o!" The opponents of Franklin Roosevelt, using the same method, got some of their best effects by crying "New Deal! New Deal! New Deal!" The phrase, by the end of Roosevelt's first term, had ceased to have any real objective meaning. It was an emotional outcry indicating, as the case might be, pleasure or pain.

A detailed examination of the "concatenation of federal actions known as the New Deal," as Charles and Mary Beard have put it, happily does not fall within the province of this essay. The economic meaning and political content of such initials as N.R.A., A.A.A., F.H.A., W.P.A., N.Y.A., and H.O.L.C. must be deciphered by a more conscientious hieroglyphist. It will be his difficult task, not only to pass judgment upon the New Deal as a social program, but also to discover what part of it may justly be attributed to Franklin Roosevelt. For whatever decision is finally struck concerning the New Deal (a decision which in large part depends upon the future drift of history) it cannot be regarded as the personal creation of the man with whom it is most intimately associated. It represents the work of many different men and many different minds, some in direct and even hostile opposition to each other, and it has not a little of the ambiguity we find in Theodore Roosevelt's "Square Deal." John Applegate has no clear idea of what it is, or any firm comprehension of the philosophy behind it. He knows, in general, that it is taken to represent "progressivism," and that Franklin Roosevelt is a "liberal," but by the middle of the Twentieth Century these terms had also come to have a purely subjective definition. Words of praise in one man's mouth, they were words of condemnation in another's. Despite this, however, a residue of concrete meaning still remained: "progressivism" indicating a willingness to try new techniques and a disinclination to return to an outmoded social status, "liberal" suggesting an emphatic insistence upon those freedoms safeguarded by the Bill of Rights and a strong sympathy for the poor and underprivileged.

The future historian, examining the various objectives of the New Deal, may find it convenient to group them under four specific headings: relief, recovery, reform, and social security. And he may see these objectives, in a more calm and objective time, as pointing toward another: the attempt to carry the nation forward to what might be called the modern stage of democratic realization——to the point, that is, where the immediate and direct interest of the state in the welfare of all its citizens, the propertyless as well as the propertied, is also recognized as essential to the democratic principle.

There will also probably be a certain surprise, indicated by those chuckling ejaculations that have become conventional with historians, that the New Deal program, which went in the direction of reform hardly further than the Liberal government of England in 1906, was looked upon as "revolutionary." It should be fairly clear, by the year 2000, that the New Deal was in direct succession to Woodrow Wilson's "New Freedom," a roughly similar program of reform which, as has been indicated, was a fruition of the hopes and ambitions of the earlier progressive movement symbolized by Theodore Roosevelt. It should also be clear that all these programs of reform were rooted in the belief of the average American that he was not getting his just share of economic consideration, and that each represented an attempt, more emphatic in the case of the New Deal than in any of the others, to make palpable that reciprocality of interest between the state and the individual citizen which is essential to the health of any society.

Then, of course, there will be the question of whether Franklin Roosevelt wanted to be a dictator. Here the chuckling ejaculations will be scattered across the page. The future historian, if he has any wit at all, will understand that the word "dictator," as used in this connection, was also an emotional outcry. When Roosevelt's critics used it they meant, not that he was truly anxious to be a Hitler or a Mussolini or a Stalin——or at least most of them did not——but that he was "a bad man": the degree of badness depending upon the degree of hostility, the element of hostility developing most generally from the critic's position in the social scale. Yet, while chuckling over his digression into semantics, the future historian, if he lives up to the earnest reputation of his guild, will recognize that the unprecedented concentration of power in the Chief Executive's hands and the ever-increasing centralization of government in Washington, brought about certain conditions which threatened to alter the whole configuration of the American system and shape its society into a substantially altered form. Nor will he fail to note that the protest against such an accumulation of power did not stem from fear and prejudice alone. He will have to point out that it went against the deepest American grain, cutting across long-established beliefs, and that, in order to defend it, an argument had to be built up that implied almost a total rejection of the American past.

He will get a certain satisfaction out of reviewing the arguments put forth by the proponents of centralized power, and, in his review, will note that the best of them, such as that of Harold Laski in *The American Presidency*, correctly point out that the American system is based upon a belief in decentralized government——a government, that is to say, whose constitutional framework was designed to prevent the development of that arbitrary and unchecked power which, in the opinion of men like Jefferson and Madison, "has destroyed the liberty and the rights of man in every government which has ever existed under the sun."

To this powerful argument, the future historian will note further, the proponents of power make no direct reply. They hold merely that a "weak" government (using an emotional adjective instead of a descriptive one) naturally seemed like a good government in the agrarian society of colonial America and that, with the coming of the Industrial Revolution and the closing of the geographical frontier, the day of the "weak" government was over. The problems of a modern industrial state—unemployment, health, housing, flood-control, etc.,—project themselves to a national scale. They must be dealt with nationally. Congress is relatively helpless in coping with them because, like the dinosaur, it is too big to be effective: it cannot devise an organic and unified approach to the problems of the times. The only answer, consequently, so the argument concludes, is a greater, not less, concentration of power in the hands of the President and those legal and extra-legal associates who act in his name. It is a "weak" government, say the proponents of power, which has always played into the hands of the propertied interests, that is an instrument of tyranny: only a "strong" government can best serve the interests of democracy.

Not having the future historian's accumulation of experience to guide us, and looking upon prophecy as beyond the function of the essay, we cannot judge what his disposal of this argument will be. It seems hardly likely, however, that he will fail to recognize it for what it is—an apology rather than an argument: a brief instead of a philosophy. This is not to say that it does not contain some shrewd and cogent observations. Congress itself would seem to be anxious to prove what Laski has called the obsolescence of federalism. But apologies, in the end, must always be influenced by personal prejudice. No one who has known a physical scientist, and a political one, will ever regard the latter as the detached and unimpassioned scientific observer he generally pretends to be.

The more recent arguments that call for an increased centralization of power in the hands of the President must be regarded as forming, in general, a brief for the Roosevelt administration. Nor can it be gainsaid that such arguments do not consider the grave problem of power, nor look before or after a particular moment in time. Another flaw in the argument for power is that it too briefly passes over the fact that when a "strong" President is needed, and a "strong" government, the American has always been ready to have one. In times of emergency he does not blink the facts. Jefferson, Jackson, Lincoln, Wilson, the two Roosevelts— all were "strong" Presidents. But winter is not summer, spring lives in a different equinox from fall. There are similar differences in political climate, and, to the democrat, one virtue of his system is that it is flexible enough to take such differences into consideration.

This does not mean that the democrat is disrespectful of those critics who hold that large reforms in the democratic system are necessary. Knowing that history is a thing in flux, and not overly anxious to fall into Hegel's error of thinking that he inhabits the ideal society, he will agree with them. He will certainly not mistake the Twentieth Century for the Eighteenth, nor deny that national problems must be attacked on a national scale. He will go even further and accept the challenge of the so-called social "impossibilitists," such as Pareto and Michels. He will agree that they are correct in saying that the actual management of government, in any society, is a function left to the relatively few. He will deny, however, that in a democracy this must inexorably make the few the master of the many, or that the many cannot exercise a substantial degree of control over the few. He will insist that the argument that calls for the concentration of all authority in a relatively small number of persons, and the passing on of such concentrated authority from administration to administration without hope or possibility of recall, is anti-democratic to the core. He will see the lesson of the first half of the Twentieth Century, in which "strong" states all over the world destroyed every vestige of democracy, as lending irrefutable support to the arguments against power brought forth by the political philosophers who believed in decentralization and contrived the American system of checks and balances. He will not be so lost in admiration of "efficiency" and "progress" as to forget the fable of King Stork.

That the future historian will look upon Franklin Roosevelt as one of the King Storks, however, seems at the moment most unlikely. A far more probable conclusion, unless the evidence accumulated during his first eleven years in office is completely swept aside, is that he will be seen as being rooted squarely and firmly in the democratic tradition——not only the leader of one of the greatest movements in American history, but, in addition, a great political educator.

It is in his achievements as an educator that Roosevelt's most enduring claim to greatness may in time be found. Of no great profundity, a political dilettante with a rather erratic and haphazard career, he came to the Presidency and the years of crisis as much in need of education as the American people; and, as he went through his process of education, reflected in his so-called "statemanship as adjustment," he carried the nation along with him. Even his enemies were forced along the way: they too, if for no other purpose than to attack, had to inquire into the nature of the forces that were shaping the destiny of the nation and the fate of the world. The 1930's in America, which the future historian may see as a time of rebirth and renewal, or an era of evidence to support Brooks Adams's grim *Law Of Civilization And Decay*, was a period of intense questioning——all things having been denied, all things had to be sought again. Was democracy possible? Did the New Deal mean socialims? Was there going to be a permanent army of unemployed? What did a planned economy mean? Did Nazism offer a threat to America? Was there going to be another War? Could the United States keep out of it? All across the land, once more turning inward upon itself for guidance and illumination, the arguments spread and flared: and, wherever the criss-crossing trails happened to lead, whatever roads the debate might follow, at the juncture of every passage stood the figure of Franklin Roosevelt. A pilgrim among other pilgrims, as much a seeker after knowledge as any of those who followed in the throng, he was always in the forefront of the search——always there was the awareness of his presence and the impact of his personality. Persisting himself, he made others persist: dramatizing Franklin Roosevelt, he dramatized the issues of his time. Politics was now more than something rural characters made salty remarks about while munching crackers around a pot-bellied stove. It lay at the center of all men's lives: there was a sense of mounting excitement in both camps——the realization that vital issues were at stake, that the very shape and content of tomorrow was in the making. Agreement or disagreement lay beside the point.

Roosevelt forced himself into the inner lives of those who opposed him as well as those who followed him——the very antagonisms he aroused, the bitterness and the hatred, all served to prove that men had been forced to abandon old

habits of thought and that Roosevelt's term of office, like that
of Jefferson and Lincoln, Jackson and Wilson, was a great
educative process. And finally, when the currents of world
revolution burst the flimsy dams that men thought might
contain them, Roosevelt came to a position of world leadership. The debates he engendered would still go on, raging
even in the midst of raging war, but now, even as in the
minds of millions the United States became *the* democracy,
Roosevelt became *the* democrat. His future reputation depends on the future's shape, upon himself and the needs of
those who come after him——each generation rewriting history to fit its own necessities——but it well may be a conclusion of the future that, having been as an educator a servant
of his age, Roosevelt, in time of war, became a servant of the
ages; raising the challenge of democracy to meet the challenge
of the New Order and himself becoming, for all the faults and
failures that may justly be laid to him, part of the democratic myth.* Posterity has not voted, and the polls of the
present are still open, but he may be found, if democracy
survives, among the enduring American memories of the
future. He is one of the major figures of a major epoch,
attracting the flashes of history as does a vein of iron in a
mountainside, and the future historian, poring over the books
with the smell of dust, dimly cloistered in his adjudicating
quiet, cannot fail to remark, perhaps with a note of regret,
that it was an adventure to live in his time.

---

* The opposite, it need hardly be said, can also happen: the future historian may have to record that, in time of war, Roosevelt's symbolic value
was obscured and that his reputation passed under a shadow from which it
never emerged.

EPILOGUE

John Applegate, American

FOR ALL the labor that will be his, as he comes to form a judgment of our time, the historian of the future is yet to be envied. Many questions will have been answered, many riddles solved. And he may be able, in the deeper concentration of a less shattered year, to come to more salient conclusions about John Applegate than any we have reached. Certain things may now be said of our rather sedentary hero, for he is still sitting in his chair by the radio——such things as, in passing, we have tried to say; that his philosophy is one of moral materialism: that he has a reverence for bigness: that he believes in personal initiative and success——but, in his identity as an American, how may he be defined except by saying that he is one who participates in the American adventure; which, suggesting everything, tells us nothing at all?

Nor are we brought any closer to the matter by saying that the adventure of America has from the beginning been the adventure of democracy, and that the American, by virtue of his participation in the adventure, is a democrat. There are some Americans who are not democrats and there are many democrats who are not Americans. The moral and spiritual principles that illumine democracy were not invented by the American——they are as deep as man's hope is deep, wide as man's fate is wide. The adventure of democracy is part of the adventure of human kind.

To say that the American is a democrat, howsoever convincing in the past, is no longer enough. Nor is celebration enough, nor evocation, nor all the purpose of poets. Democracy, as a faith in battle against other faiths, is itself on trial.

It and the American have gone down to the furnace together. The one cannot endure without the other. Democracy would not have been the same without the American and the American would not have been the same without democracy. They must both endure or be melted down. For without a belief in democracy, and in those moral and spiritual principles on which such belief is based——that man has worth and dignity: that the state is a means to the ends of man: that as rational and spiritual beings all men are equal, mutually participating in the communion of the human species——without the inspiration of these beliefs the American adventure has no meaning. Democracy becomes but another way of arranging the affairs of society. It must then be tested by its utility and efficiency. It becomes a machine, and man a cog in the machine, and the ends of the machine are not the ends of man. And, should this happen, the American will have lost some of his meaning. Democracy will not be the same without the American and the American will not be the same without democracy.

The American and his faith are on trial together. It is not democracy that makes the faith but the faith that makes democracy. The faith is there or it is not there. Exhortations will not call it forth, nor thunderings, nor all the wailings by the wall. It is there or it is not there. The American goes down to the furnace and he takes his faith with him. The armed and the armor are equally tested.

What does the American bring to the testing? What is his armor as he meets the trial?

He brings his memory and the memories that are part of memory. He is armed with a love of his native place. The sounds of the states are part of memory, the names of the cities and the towns, the sun on the peaks and the shadow of clouds in the valleys beyond the peaks. There are other cities and other towns: there are peaks and valleys he has never seen. His are no better, no richer, perhaps less fair than most

——but his. They are part of his own country. Memory and love are brought to the testing.

He brings his willingness to adventure. His fathers uprooted themselves from their native soils for many reasons, noble and ignoble, but merely to forswear the known for the unknown, whatever the impulse, is an act of high courage. These were the adventurers, in the cattleboat as in the *Mayflower*, and the American is the son of adventurers. Generally considered a "conservative," which correctly means one who wants to preserve the best values of the past, the American is perhaps the conservative's opposite: it may be that he cares too little, instead of too much, for traditional values. He likes things because they are modern, and is fascinated by newness, and such hope as he has for the future is based largely on the belief that tomorrow will be more streamlined than today——it will be a fine thing, he tells himself, to fly to Buenos Aires for the week-end instead of motoring to the usual hills or shore.

He brings to the testing his belief in tomorrow. The very largeness of his country, the bigness that the American delights in, did much to confirm this belief. In the beginning there was the wilderness, stretching from shore to shore, and the wilderness and the future were as one——the promise of tomorrow lay always to the west. And should the promise fail, should drought parch dream and flood drown hope, then still the western future beckoned——tomorrow must be better than today.

Memory, love, optimism, the willingness to adventure—— all these he brings to the testing. He also brings his philosophy of moral materialism. The American, finding his identity in the wilderness, also found an emptiness. He could fire his rifle and not be heard: he could ride for miles and not be seen: he could paddle for days and meet no other canoe. He was alone, lost in the new immensity, and he shed the trappings of his European inheritance as a blacksnake sheds its skin. He lived

a new kind of life, begot a new kind of language, became a new kind of man. The time of celebration was not yet, nor the years of defamation, but he knew his newness and his condition and that this was different from the past. He was a new man in a new world and he was free. He came to his freedom before he came to his independence, hewing it out of the wilderness even as he hewed the logs he notched to fit his cabin's shape, and after he was free, and himself a document of independence, he wrote his charter and flung his challenge to the world.

The moral and spiritual principles contained in his declaration of independence he did not puzzle much. Learning was not his trade, and the rhythm of an axe-head no metronome to philosophy, and metaphysics a thing beyond him. Besides, there was work to do. The emptiness had to be filled up.

The emptiness was moral as well as physical. As the pioneer slipped his past, so were his sons to slip their past, and the sons of their sons after them. The lessons of the Puritans were taken into the wilderness, and next to the schoolhouse was built the church, but with so much work to do, and so much to be gained by work, the fiery gospel of the theocratic fathers, shot with terror and mystery and the awesome anger of God, became less and less a religion of the inner life and more and more a doctrine of getting ahead——do something, be somebody, get somewhere in the world. This is a kind of idealism, and a driving force in American life, but in the end the ideal becomes not work for the sake of work, not craft for the sake of craft, but work and craft for the sake of the material gain work and craft will bring.

The American brings his materialism to the testing, his desire for a higher standard of living, his general idea that all the ills of the world may be cured by larger and larger applications of goods. He brings that part of himself that found its worst reflection in Huey Long, and its best in those acts of public and private good-will that may be seen as examples of practical Christianity——more works, in large, than faith. He brings his belief in the success story, and in the sound that money makes, and in the things that money can buy.

With his materialism he brings his idealism. Whether the one or the other is larger in his character only the testing can tell. But the idealism, because of the materialism, cannot be denied. Idealism as a force in America, it may be said, reached its culmination just before the Civil War and then, after the war, gave way to the pragmatism that sought to endow the materialistic drift of American life with some kind of purpose. But even the dinosaurian capitalists represented by Andrew Carnegie had to find idealistic excuses for their material points of view——read their autobiographies; look at the foundations, the libraries, the college-buildings——and if the idealism was used merely as a cloth to polish the materialism into something brighter than it was, at least there was the admission and understanding that it would cause things to look a little better in their neighbors' eyes.

The American fought two wars in which idealism was involved, one to free the slaves and one to free the world, and if after the conflicts were over he lapsed into a deeper preoccupation with material enterprise and worldly success, if the modern cynic came blandly to assume that the moral world was simply an illusion and that its values did not exist, that good and evil refer to that which is good and evil for a particular organism at a particular point in time, that idealism is a snare and a delusion——in spite of this, idealism persisted and those who worked in idealism's name. A large part of the New Deal, it will be noted, was objected to because of the idealism it contained and also because it gathered within its fold too many dreamers and mystics and poets——those who thought that were man's burden of living eased a little he might pause for a moment and know the wonder of being alive; and perhaps, in the knowing, lift his attention to things that were good and fine in themselves: such things as give the life of Abraham Lincoln more than ordinary meaning and make him one of the most haunting moments in the conscience of man.

The American goes down to the furnace and he takes all things with him. The tares are bundled with the wheat, the failures with the triumph. How he shall return from the furnace, shaping his future and the world's future——for shape it he must, whether or no, acting or not acting——only the later historian can know. This scholar (will he be one of the peoples of Asia, perhaps?) may follow the American's path downward to the decadent imperialism of the modern feudal state, and thus write a halt to the American adventure, or, again, he may see him fallen under the shadow of one of those long nights that sometimes darken that which we so grimly persist in calling civilization.

We prefer to think, however, that his will be a happier task and that, in even so slender a reed as John Applegate, he may find an answer to the prophets of decay who will doubtless be as mournful in his time as they are in ours. For what these prophets forget, in their fixation with collective tendencies, is that moral choices are open to individuals. It cannot be predicted that John Applegate will choose the good, the beautiful, the true, any more than that he will choose the false, the cruel, the ugly. But the chance for choice is there and the nature of the choice must necessarily be influenced by his inheritance and, because it is part of his inheritance, the measure of his democratic faith. He believes or he does not believe: he affirms or he does not affirm.

It is quite useless to harry or browbeat him. He is a man, his character has been formed, his human nature will not be changed at the crack of a pistol-shot. He will pay but little attention to those who tell him what he must or must not do. He has lost his fear of hell-fire and he still thinks that, come what may, he can master the raw material of tomorrow and bend the future to its proper shape. With so much confidence, there is room for confidence: with so much good in his past, and in himself, there must be good in his future——not all good, any more than all evil: good and evil all bound together, as in the contradiction that is man, and if the world is lucky, very lucky, the measure of evil less than the measure of good.

But the largeness of his future, in the end, can be no larger than his faith in those moral and spiritual values that give more than a political meaning to democracy. If democracy has only a political meaning, if it is to be measured merely by its efficiency, it must be judged as a machine is judged——and what a clumsy, complicated, inefficient machine democracy is at times. Why expect John Applegate or his son, who belongs to the generation of the fox-holes, to defend it? They have an American dislike for things that do not work. Their very liking for what is new and modern and efficient might make them all the more willing to change.

Any defence of democracy must finally be based on the faith that democracy implies——a belief in those abstract truths, not any more American than life is American, or death American, which, as Lincoln said, make the Declaration of Independence more than a mere revolutionary document. The document, itself, is not enough: not any more today than in the beginning. It is the abstract truths that were written into the document, its moral and ethical inspiration, that make it possible for democracy to be seen as a bridgehead to the future. Not because it is the American form of government, or even the best form of government, (as, of course, it is) but because only its breadth of spirit is large enough to contain the possible largeness of the future. Such inspiration, belonging together to all men, make it possible for all men to be drawn together. The community of man did not need the airplane to bridge the distances. Men have been neighbors, in this community, long before the physical shrinking of the world.

The airplane, which as a determining factor is to the Twentieth Century what the steam-engine was to the Nineteenth, will not create the world community. It can, at best, merely create proximity. And proximity is proximity—nothing else. It does not make for justice, or mercy, or virtue, or a belief in reason, or loving-kindness, or any of those other things upon which the hope of a world community must depend. Proximity will not make neighbors of those who are not neighbors. The airplane is a machine and it has the machine's indifference. All places are equal in the bombsight's eyes. The hope of man's community must rest on something else. There needs must be, along with proximity in space, a certain proximity in spacelessness—a mutual sharing of belief. Without such mutuality the neighborhood is no neighborhood. It becomes a collection of targets.

But any prediction, in this regard, involves a matter of hope. And what can we hope for the American, for John Applegate, other than that the historian of the future will find that he marked a beginning and an end: that he came to a door and opened the door: that in the testing he both found and lost himself, knowing his identity as one man and his greater identity as one man among all men, and that, after the time of the furnace, the time of promise was come again. To hope less would be to wish him less. To hope more—well, who dares?

Pisgah Forest, N. C., August, 1941
South Hadley Center, Mass., July, 1943

INDEX

AN ACKNOWLEDGMENT

This book, like most of its kind, has borrowed from many others. I have tried, throughout the text, to indicate the sources of such borrowing, seeing no reason why plagiarism should be confessed in the small voice of footnotes, but beyond this I owe a particular debt to George Santayana's *Character and Opinion in the United States* and Charles and Mary Beard's *The Rise of American Civilization.*

I would like to thank Mr. Van Wyck Brooks, Mr. Bernard de Voto, Mr. Edgar Lee Masters and Mr. Edmund Wilson for permission to quote from their books, and I am under a special obligation to Mr. Newton McKeon and Mr. Anthony Scenna of the Amherst College Library, without whose generous assistance much of the research need for this volume would have been impossible.

H. B.